KIDS
COME IN ALL
LANGUAGES

KIDS
COME IN ALL
LANGUAGES

Visible Learning® for Multilingual Learners

OSCAR CORRIGAN

NANCY FREY

DOUGLAS FISHER

JOHN HATTIE

FOR INFORMATION:

Corwin

A SAGE Company

2455 Teller Road

Thousand Oaks, California 91320

(800) 233-9936

www.corwin.com

SAGE Publications Ltd.

1 Oliver's Yard

55 City Road

London EC1Y 1SP

United Kingdom

SAGE Publications India Pvt. Ltd.

Unit No 323-333, Third Floor, F-Block

International Trade Tower Nehru Place

New Delhi 110 019

India

SAGE Publications Asia-Pacific Pte. Ltd.

18 Cross Street #10-10/11/12

China Square Central

Singapore 048423

President: Mike Soules

Vice President and
  Editorial Director: Monica Eckman

Director and Publisher,
  Corwin Classroom: Lisa Luedeke

Associate Content Development
  Editor: Sarah Ross

Editorial Assistant: Madison Nevin

Production Editor: Melanie Birdsall

Typesetter: C&M Digitals (P) Ltd.

Proofreader: Jeff Bryant

Cover Designer: Janet Kiesel

Marketing Manager: Megan Naidl

Printed in the United States of America

ISBN 978-1-5443-4148-4

Library of Congress Control Number: 2023936229

This book is printed on acid-free paper.

23 24 25 26 27 10 9 8 7 6 5 4 3 2 1

Contents

Acknowledgments   vii

Introduction   1

Chapter 1. Learning About Multilingual Learners   5

The Changing Face of Schools   7

Successful Systems for Multilingual Learners   8

The Role of Expectations for Multilingual Learners   10

Knowing Our Students   12

Warning: Multilingual Learners Are Not a Monolithic Group   14

Marking the Development of Multilingual Learners   15

Conclusion   16

Chapter 2. Climate for Learning   17

Belonging   18

Peers Helping Peers   20

Setting the Physical Environment   22

Classroom Agreements   25

Grouping Students   27

Conclusion   30

Chapter 3. Challenge as Learning   31

Designing Complex Tasks   36

Persistence and Resilience   40

Use Language That Encourages Persistence   40

Conclusion   43

Chapter 4. Clarity of Learning   45

Enter Teacher Clarity   46

Start With What Success Looks Like   48

Design Daily Learning Intentions and Success Criteria   50

Find the Relevance   58

Conclusion   59

Chapter 5. Cohesion in Learning   61

Quality Core Instruction for Multilingual Learners   62

Focused Instruction for Multilingual Learners   63

Modeling and Demonstrating in a Contrastive
Grammar Lesson   65

Guided Instruction for Multilingual Learners   67

Collaborative Learning for Multilingual Learners   70

Independent Learning for Multilingual Learners   74

Conclusion   76

Chapter 6. Checks Into Learning   79

Informing Instruction   81

Implementing an Assessment System   83

Oral Language   86

Tests   93

Effective Assessment Practices   96

Conclusion   97

Final Thoughts   99

Appendix: Student Oral Language Observation Matrix (SOLOM)   **101**

References   **105**

Index   **111**

Acknowledgments

Corwin gratefully acknowledges the contributions of the following reviewers:

Melissa Black
Elementary Educator and Education Consultant
DCPS

Andrea Honigsfeld
TESOL Professor
Molloy University

Darius Phelps
Adjunct Literacy Instructor, Poet, and Classroom Teacher
Teachers College, Columbia University,
   CUNY Queens/Hunter College

Introduction

This is a Visible Learning® book. And it's a book about multilingual learners. In this introduction, we'll explore what we mean by these two ideas. First, multilingual learners. We use the term *multilingual learner,* a more contemporary designation for students who are adding English to their language and literacy skills (e.g., González-Howard & Suárez, 2021). Others suggest *emergent bilingual,* emphasizing the value of bilingualism. Noting that "giving someone or a group of people a name is a political act," González-Howard and Suárez (2021) remind educators that labels and naming are "intimately connected to our ideologies, assumptions, and goals for students and who they can become" (p. 749). The word *multilingual* rightly positions learning as an additive, whereas *English learner* (EL) can reinforce a deficit mindset that highlights what a student can't do. It may be this deficit mindset that has thwarted efforts to improve the outcomes for multilingual learners (S. H. Wang et al., 2021). Further, the term *multilingual* has been used for decades, first by ethnologists to describe communities where more than one language is used, and later by linguists to highlight learning processes.

Educators of multilingual learners should recognize the following:

1. Multilingual learners are a diverse group with individual needs that can be addressed by understanding proficiency levels and holding reasonable expectations (Zacarian, 2023).

2. Multilingual learners are doubly challenged, as they must learn English while learning *in* English (Short & Fitzsimmons, 2007). They benefit from quality instructional programs that emphasize student talk to give them lots of experiences using academic language.

> Assessment for multilingual learners should highlight strengths and not simply catalog deficits.

3. Assessment for multilingual learners requires attention to the whole child. This multidimensional approach is necessary for a true picture to emerge. It requires balancing large-scale assessments with individualized, informal ones that highlight strengths and do not simply catalog deficits (Gottlieb, 2021).

4. Response to instruction and intervention with multilingual learners is complex because of the many factors that influence subsequent-language development. Multilingual learners deserve supplemental and intensive interventions, especially when their performance is not on track with true peers' (Fisher et al., 2011).

Know What Works in Education

It's important to recognize that, as a field, at times we have learned about what works by experiencing what doesn't work. Those unsuccessful efforts have heightened our sense of what we already know works in classrooms (Hattie, 2023):

- Fostering student self-regulation is crucial for moving learning to deep and transfer levels.

- Learning accelerates when the student, not the teacher, is in control of learning.

- There needs to be a diversity of instructional approaches (not just some direct instruction and then some independent work).

- Well-designed peer learning impacts understanding.

- Feedback in a high-trust environment must be integrated into the learning cycle.

Learning accelerates when the student, not the teacher, is in control of learning.

A significant amount of published research about education exists, and more studies are produced each year. Who doesn't want to make research- or evidence-based decisions about teaching and learning? Yet it's often hard to sift through the vast amounts of research material to figure out what to do. At times, it seems that everything "works," so any choice we make seems reasonable. But the fact of the matter is that some things work best. Thus, knowing what works best to accelerate students' learning is useful.

Enter the Visible Learning database (www.visiblelearningmetax.com), which represents the largest summary of educational research ever conducted. This database focuses on meta-analyses, or aggregations of studies, to determine the impact that specific actions or influences have on students' learning. In other words, the database offers studies of studies, intending to identify patterns that can inform the collective work of teachers and leaders. The database currently includes more than 2100 meta-analyses with more than 500 million students.

These meta-analyses use effect size to scale the impact. Hattie's analyses of these meta-analyses are reported using this quantitative statistical tool to measure the magnitude, or size, of a given influence. An effect size of $d = 0.0$ indicates that no change in achievement is related to the intervention. An effect size of $d = 1.0$ indicates an increase in one standard deviation on the outcome. A $d = 1.0$ is typically associated with advancing students' achievement by about two years, meaning that, on average, the achievement of students would exceed that of 84 percent of those who did not receive the treatment. In other words, the potential for acceleration is substantial. From this data, Hattie has identified 350 influences on student learning.

The average impact of those 350 influences is 0.40. Thus, influences over 0.40 are above the average and have the potential to accelerate students' learning. Those below 0.40 are less likely to ensure that students learn a full year of material for a year of school. That does not mean we ignore those influences below 0.40, but rather we are cautious about those influences' link to student achievement, which is often cited as the justification for why something is done. For example, modifying the school calendar to alter the summer vacation schedule has an effect size of 0.09, meaning it has a small potential to accelerate learning. In this example, there may be other legitimate reasons for altering the school calendar, but improving student achievement shouldn't be used as a justification for doing so.

Let's consider a few more examples. You may have observed that a student's prior achievement is related to their future achievement; the research shows that the effect size is 0.73. Students who have achieved in the past are likely to achieve in the future on related subject matter. This finding also speaks to the value of knowing students well in order to link prior knowledge to new knowledge.

Similarly, no doubt you have observed that boredom has a negative effect on learning. The effect size is actually −0.46. Learning opportunities are lost when students are bored, which can occur when they fail to perceive the relevance or are overwhelmed by information they can't access.

Influences over 0.40 are above the average and have the potential to accelerate students' learning.

Several themes are at the heart of Visible Learning:

1. **Investment in learning means there is a drive to foster each student's increasing ability to recognize when they are learning or when they are not and how to fix it**. Teacher clarity and feedback are crucial. In this book, you will find chapters devoted to these two things.

2. **Teachers know the impact of their instruction in terms of progress and achievement and take steps to refine their approaches**. That means that we have methods for discovering what students already know to minimize wasted instructional time so that we can focus on needed learning experiences. Further, the individual student is the unit of analysis—we know what works, what works when, and what works for whom. When something is not working, we change it to obtain the desired impact.

3. **The mindframes of teachers—their dispositions and beliefs—are in the driver's seat**. That means we collaborate, talk about learning more than we talk about teaching, and invest in relationships with children and adults to be an agent of change. In fact, the way we think about our teaching is critical, and this book is designed to support your thinking as an effective educator of multilingual learners.

> This book is designed to support your thinking as an effective educator of multilingual learners.

Organization of the Book

This book is different because it mobilizes the evidence from Visible Learning and focuses that evidence on multilingual learners. Based on the evidence, we have organized the information in a Five C instructional framework:

- Climate for learning
- Challenge as learning
- Clarity of learning
- Cohesion in learning
- Checks into learning

This framework ensures that educators provide multilingual learners with the best equitable learning environment to be successful. Although we present these as individual standards, in reality they are interconnected and interrelated. The following chapters will explore these big ideas and provide practical information about how to implement them in schools to help all our students thrive.

Learning About Multilingual Learners

1

Big Idea

Multilingual learners are a diverse group with individual needs that can be addressed by understanding proficiency levels and students' complex personal and academic experiences while holding high expectations for students as they are developing proficiency and learning content.

Questions Educators Ask

- What are the characteristics of multilingual learners?

- What are the components of a successful system of support for multilingual learners?

- What role do teacher expectations play in the education of multilingual learners?

- What do you need to know about your multilingual learners as they develop language, literacy, and content knowledge?

We fled Afghanistan, leaving everything behind as we made our way to Pakistan. The 12-hour trip in the back of a truck took two days and nights. We climbed mountains, crawled through dirt caves, and hid from certain torture and death. With no food and little water, my mother, brother, and I reached Pakistan and wandered the streets for days. After many desperate months, my mother got a job that barely paid for our room. Although we went many nights without food, I had no time to focus on how bad my situation was because my priority was to do well in school and learn Urdu. Education had become my refuge and, once again, my joy in life.

While living in Pakistan for 7 years, we faced many challenges and obstacles. I even stopped going to school because it got too hard to keep my grades up and to pay attention in my classes. I started working in order to support my family. Sometimes I used to see students coming from school. Tears fell from my eyes, and I used to say to myself how great it feels when you go to school and learn new things every day. I used to think that I would never return to school or become the person I had dreamed of.

Then, an amazing event changed my life. After an extensive interview and a home visit from a United Nations High Commissioner for Refugees officials, my mother, my brother, and I were allowed to fly to America. A journey of two nights and three days placed us on American soil, in the city of Boise, Idaho.

The next morning was a true awakening. Slowly, the darkness that had stretched from the night of my father's and brother's deaths began to lighten, and I faced each new challenge eagerly. My biggest obstacle was learning English, so I worked hard in class, read more than my friends, listened to the news every night, and spoke English every chance I could. I got help from teachers and friends, who became my mentors and role models.

Now I see my life's path as a circle that I began to walk the day I arrived in America, when individuals opened their hearts to me, and opportunities—like open arms—embraced me. I will widen this circle as I reach out to others to make a difference in their lives.

—Arian Dyanat

Think of yourself so eager to have an education but not able to attend school. Imagine living in constant violence, destruction, and war where you lose one or more of your beloved family members. Your family is torn apart, running away to survive, and you are only twelve years old. Yes, it is hard to imagine, but I have lived through it all. Members of my family escaped Ethiopia's tyrannical regime, only to face more terror in Kenya as refugees. We never gave up hope for finding peace and freedom and, with determination, finally found a new home in the USA. I still carry my past with me; it is impossible to forget, and it has taught me valuable life lessons about positive leadership and the importance of building community. The obstacles I overcame have helped me develop determination and persistence in any challenge I now face.

"The journey of a thousand miles begins with a single step." I keep this quote in my mind as I keep my family in Africa in my heart. And I believe that my mind and heart will continue to guide me, just one individual, to make this world a better place.

—Abdurashid Ali

The journeys of these two extraordinary young people, in their own words, can teach us much about what is possible in the face of seemingly insurmountable obstacles. Their journeys can teach us much about ourselves as teachers and as learners in our own journey toward high standards and high achievement for all our students.

This journey begins with two steps—knowing our students and knowing where we are going. Effective teachers are in a constant cycle of assessing, planning, teaching, and reflecting. Knowing your students means knowing their language and literacy levels and their skill in writing. It also means knowing about their prior schooling, literacy in their primary language, and the circumstances of their arrival in this country. It means recognizing how the structures of their primary language and the worldview of their culture impact their comprehension, learning, and use of English. And it means knowing their strengths, assets, talents, passions, and interests.

For teachers of multilingual learners, knowing where you are going means having a clear definition of what it means to be proficient in a language, as well as knowledge of language, language learning, and language teaching. Let's begin with knowing our students—who are our multilingual learners?

The Changing Face of Schools

The population of U.S. public school students learning English as an additional language has increased dramatically since the turn of this century. The National Center for Education Statistics reported in 2019 (the last year of reporting at the date of this publication) that the number of multilingual learners in grades K–12 had grown from 9.2 percent, or 4.5 million students in 2010, to 10.4 percent, or 5.1 million students. Multilingual learners in the United States hail from all over the world. The majority (75.9 percent) speak Spanish as a first language, and the second most common language in the fall of 2019 was Arabic (National Center for Education Statistics, 2022).

Twelve states now report that multilingual learners exceed 10 percent of their student population. California, Texas, New York, and Illinois have the largest numbers of students who are learning English as an additional language, but Alaska, Colorado, Delaware, Maryland, Nevada, New Mexico, Rhode Island, and Washington have joined the ranks of those educating a significant number of multilingual learners.

Sadly, the academic learning and linguistic progress of multilingual learners has remained problematic despite many efforts to improve student learning outcomes. Despite many initiatives designed to improve student outcomes, the achievement of multilingual learners is essentially flat. For example, the New York State Education Department reported in 2021 that the four-year graduation rate for multilingual learners was 61 percent compared to 91 percent for all other students (New York State Education Department, 2021). Many multilingual learners who enter the U.S. school system during adolescence believe there is no way for them to pass the tests required under state mandates. According to Child Trends (Murphy, 2014), at the national level, just under one-third of English language learner (ELL) students (31 percent) scored at the basic level or above in reading in fourth grade, compared with more than two-thirds (72 percent) of non-ELL students.

> Sadly, the academic learning and linguistic progress of multilingual learners has remained problematic despite many efforts to improve student learning outcomes.

According to the U.S. Department of Education,

> In grade 4, roughly the same number of states experienced increases as states that experienced decreases in the percentage of ELs [English learners] proficient in reading. Nine states experienced essentially no change from 2009 to 2017. Overall, the percentage of ELs proficient in reading rose by 3 percentage points in grade 4 (from 6 percent to 9 percent) and by 2 percentage points in grade 8 (from 3 percent to 5 percent). (U.S. Department of Education, n.d.)

Successful Systems for Multilingual Learners

Successful systems for multilingual learners do not leave support for learning to chance. For example, the World-class Instructional Design and Assessment (WIDA) has articulated four "big ideas" foundational to serving learners well (WIDA, 2020, p. 17). These four big ideas are related to

- **EQUITY** of Opportunity and Access

- **COLLABORATION** Among Stakeholders

- **INTEGRATION** of Content and Language

- **FUNCTIONAL APPROACH** to Language Development

Let's briefly explore each big idea in more detail.

Equity of Opportunity and Access

This first principle serves as a foundation for the others that follow. Opportunity to learn (OTL) was discussed by Coleman et al. (1966) and has since been expanded by others across several dimensions: instructional time, content or subject matter, and degree of complexity of skills and concepts. Systematic exposure to less-challenging curriculum results in depressed achievement: For so many topics, students simply can't learn what they haven't been taught.

Equity of opportunity works in tandem with access to high-quality curriculum and instruction. It isn't just about the ability to enroll in a course; it is a matter of what actually happens inside that classroom. A successful approach includes scaffolded language supports; it also involves the practice of translanguaging—encouraging students to use their full range of experiences and communication modes—instead of viewing English as the only path to learning (e.g., Lewis et al., 2012). Translanguaging does not require that the teacher can speak the same heritage language as the learner; instead, it advocates for teachers to move from a "monoglossic" belief to one that leverages multimodal approaches for text, visuals, and cultural knowledge to promote learning (García, 2020).

Systematic exposure to less-challenging curriculum results in depressed achievement: Students simply can't learn what they haven't been taught.

Collaboration Among Stakeholders

The successful education of multilingual learners requires meaningful collaboration among professionals and the students' families. In terms of the professionals, this requires regular consultation among content teachers, language specialists, and school administrators (WIDA, 2020). But even these essential collaborations are diminished if families and the larger community are not seen as important resources. The ability to leverage students' assets will not be possible if teachers don't know what those assets are. And sharing the same language as the students does not mean that educators understand what the children bring socioculturally—or their identities. For decades, the field has understood the crucial function of funds of knowledge in positioning learning relationships between home and school (Moll et al., 1992).

Integration of Content and Language

The need to communicate permeates everything we do, not only in the classroom but also beyond its walls. Thus, teachers must ensure they have addressed the linguistic—not just the academic—demands of the content or task. In other words, we must analyze every lesson for the linguistic opportunities provided for students. Teachers, especially those who were not multilingual learners in school, need to be reminded that multilingual learners are doing double the work: They are tasked with learning content and language simultaneously (Short & Fitzsimmons, 2007).

Functional Approach to Language Development

The function of communication determines the form that it takes. Halliday (1976) stated that the need for language, and therefore the motivator for developing it, lies in its function. He categorized these into four areas:

The successful education of multilingual learners requires meaningful collaboration among professionals and the students' families.

- **Instrumental**, as when expressing a need ("I want a drink of water")
- **Regulatory**, as when telling someone else what to do ("Give me that")
- **Interactional**, to engage in conversation and build relationships ("I like you")
- **Personal**, to express feelings, opinions, and identity ("I am happy")

These basic functions of language are transformed in school settings through speaking and writing. Folding the functions of the language needed in the classroom with the content illuminates the tools students need.

The Role of Expectations for Multilingual Learners

Teacher expectations play a significant role in the education of multilingual learners (Canillas, 2021; Pit-ten Cate & Glock, 2018; Rubie-Davies & Peterson, 2016; Stutzman & Lowenhaupt, 2022; S. Wang et al., 2018). Far too often, teachers hold their multilingual learners to lower standards, accept inferior work, and attribute students' proficiency levels and lack of achievement to students' demographics, including ethnicity and social class (Nora & Echevarria, 2016). This clearly contributes to the limited progress multilingual learners have made over the past several decades.

In fact, teacher expectations have an influence on students' learning. An effect size is a statistical tool for measuring the magnitude of an influence. Teacher expectations have been demonstrated to influence learning, with an effect size of 0.42 (www.visiblelearningmetax.com). In the words of Glass, an effect size not only addresses the question "does a treatment affect people"; it also reveals the answer to "how much does it affect them" (quoted in Kline, 2004, p. 95). There was a discussion of effect size in the introduction; remember that an effect size of 0.42 means that it holds the potential to accelerate learning.

And *potential* is the key term in that last sentence. Teacher expectations may be accurate, or they may be low due to biases. The further entanglement of language, ethnicity, race, and economic status results in some stark outcomes, and these biases, expressed as teacher expectations, influence what students are taught or not taught. A study of 150,000 classrooms examined the literacy experiences of those serving at least 20 percent of multilingual learners (TNTP, 2022). They found that one-third of the articles and paired texts assigned to students were below grade level. Notably, the study included years impacted by the pandemic, from 2018 to 2021. The authors stated, "Inequities in access to grade-level work that existed long before the pandemic have only deepened, and . . . most school systems are not yet implementing strategies that could put students on track to recover from the disruption of the last several years" (p. 2).

These lower expectations are often manifested in subtle ways, even as teachers themselves believe their expectations for their multilingual learners are just as high as those of their other students. Their intentions are admirable: they don't want to embarrass the students by asking questions that require the expression of a complete thought, frustrate them by giving them a difficult assignment, or inhibit them by correcting errors. The outcome, however, is often that multilingual learners are not exposed to grade-level curriculum and are not held accountable for the same level of performance as native English speakers. Rubie-Davies' (2014) work on teacher expectations reveals that those with lower expectations routinely accept an inferior standard of work. A simple exchange between a teacher and a student can hold the student to high standards or allow them to sit in silence and become a passive learner while the teacher turns to another student for the answer.

Teacher expectations extend to their expectations about their students' families, too. Educators too often mistakenly underestimate the capacity of multilingual parents to help their children succeed in school. Wassell et al. (2017) investigated the expectations of middle school STEM (science, technology, engineering, and mathematics) teachers serving many multilingual learners. They found that although the teachers in the study acknowledged the importance of communication and professed empathy for the socioeconomic challenges and limited formal education faced by some families, they held to a narrow conception of what they termed "good parents" and "bad parents." In the teachers' description, "good parents" attended conferences and school events and helped with homework. "Bad parents" did not, and therefore those parents were assumed to not care about their child's education. Even as the teachers acknowledged communication factors with families as a barrier, their practices and expectations contradicted their stated beliefs. In practice, they held the

> Far too often, teachers hold their multilingual learners to lower standards and attribute students' proficiency levels and lack of achievement to students' demographics.

same expectations for family involvement in home-school communication and assistance with homework as they did for English-proficient families.

Parents of multilingual learners express both the willingness and the ability to support their children's learning (August & Shanahan, 2006). And the evidence is that parents' expectations and aspirations for their child hold an effect size of 0.70, meaning that they have considerable potential to accelerate student achievement (Hattie & Hattie, 2022; www.visiblelearningmetax.com). However, cross-cultural communication barriers can get in the way of parents effectively partnering with educators. A study focused on parents of children enrolled in an elementary dual language program revealed that many Spanish-speaking parents saw their involvement as crucial to their child's success but expressed concerns about communicating with the school, including a lack of personnel other than teachers in the dual language program who spoke Spanish. They found this to be an impediment to their child's success, noting "that their children would learn more knowing that [their families] are accepted and embraced by the school community" (Gerena, 2011, p. 359). In addition, they had questions about how their child's heritage language was being maintained, as they viewed this as critical to maintaining family relationships and communication at home. These concerns, it should be stated, are rarely addressed in educators' work with the families of multilingual children.

> Educators too often mistakenly underestimate the capacity of multilingual parents to help their children succeed in school.

Knowing Our Students

Knowing our multilingual students as learners, of course, means that we know their proficiency levels in English and literacy skills and that we know what background knowledge, interests, passions, and lived experiences they bring to the specific content we are teaching. The adult-child relationship is a personal one that involves knowing about our students' lives, their families, and their backgrounds. Further, the effect size of student expectations is much larger than that for teachers and parents at 1.33. If multilanguage students believe they cannot learn and are not smart, this is a powerful impediment to their success. Ensuring multilingual students reach their potential is critical, as the educators' role is to help students exceed what they think is their potential. Knowledge about our students allows us to bridge the gap between school and the world where our students live, a world that often differs from the world of school. Knowing our students as children or as adolescents allows us to draw upon their funds of knowledge (Moll et al., 1992), integrating what they already know and understand with grade-level content. It is evident that we must take the necessary steps to create a welcoming, caring, supportive learning environment for our multilingual learners. Thankfully, there is evidence for what works and what doesn't, which can support us as we strive to help our multilingual students reach high levels of success.

There are some similarities between first- and second-language, or subsequent-language, learning. How do infants acquire their first language? They receive immense amounts of input from the people around them. They hear language over and over again, all day, for years. Likewise, they see many clues around them to help connect the words to actions, things, and ideas. No one minds if they make mistakes as they learn to speak. Caregivers often model the correct way to express a thought simply by restating it. Babies are rewarded with praise and encouragement for their efforts. They use language to communicate with others about their world all day. And there is always a real-life purpose for the communication.

> Knowledge about our students allows us to bridge the gap between school and the world where our students live.

With that in mind, second-language acquisition for school-aged children has some unique features that are worth attending to. These show the importance of teachers creating nurturing classroom cultures, as well as the importance of language, language, and more language:

1. **Comprehensible input:** Multilingual learners need to hear language that is comprehensible to them throughout the day (Krashen, 1986).

2. **Comprehensible output:** Multilingual learners need opportunities to communicate in the target language to encounter gaps, and then can repair those gaps to make their message understood by others (Swain, 1985).

3. **Interaction:** Multilingual learners need to use language with others for authentic purposes (Long, 1990).

4. **Low-anxiety environment:** Multilingual learners need to feel psychologically safe enough to make mistakes and take risks (Edmondson, 1999).

An important difference comes into play when additional language learning takes place in school, where individual attention is infrequent and grade-level content must be learned at the same time as language. In this situation, it becomes essential that we provide explicit, focused language instruction, along with scaffolds (support) to make content learning accessible to students who are still learning the language. In other words, systematic instruction in language acquisition is import-ant, as are opportunities for students to use academic language to talk and write about academic concepts.

To enact WIDA's principles of sound systems of support, the climate for learning, the clarity of the learning, and the cohesion of learning are always in play. The process of a system of supports begins with the identification and classification of a multilingual learner, and the remainder of this chapter is dedicated to those processes and procedures. Each of the Five Cs can and should be woven into the fabric of the initial assessment and classification process, a task that requires intentionality from our first contact with the multilingual student and their family.

Warning: Multilingual Learners Are Not a Monolithic Group

One of the most important things to recognize about teaching multilingual learners is that they are not a monolithic group. One of the best ways to describe multilingual learners is to acknowledge their diversity, as they differ in several important ways, including the following:

> One of the most important things to recognize about teaching multilingual learners is that they are not a monolithic group.

- **Linguistic.** While Spanish is the second most common language in the United States, students in a given school district might speak more than one hundred different languages. These languages differ in their pronunciation patterns, orthographic representations, and histories, and thus in the ease with which students can transfer their prior knowledge about language to the process of learning English. The more different a student's primary language is from English, the greater the challenge in transferring their knowledge about language to English.

- **Proficiency in the home language.** Based on a number of factors, including age and prior education, students who speak the same language and are the same age may have very different levels of academic language proficiency in their home language. The development of a formal first language facilitates learning in additional languages. Some students are bilingual, meaning that they speak two languages, whereas others are biliterate, meaning that they read and write proficiently in both languages.

- **Generation.** There are recognized differences in language proficiency for students of different generations living in the United States. First and second generations of multilingual learners differ from each other in significant ways, including the ability to use English at home. Evidence on generation 1.5 students (protracted multilingual learners born within or outside the United States) suggests that these students attempt to straddle their old world and the new world in which they live, and thus they experience greater difficulty in developing English proficiency.

- **Number of languages spoken.** Some students enroll in U.S. schools having mastered more than one language already, so they may have previously gained linguistic flexibility that can aid them in learning additional languages. In contrast, others may have spoken one language at home for years, so their exposure to English is a new learning experience.

- **Motivation.** Often tied in with their migration, immigration, or birthplace, students differ in their motivation to learn English. Immigrant families leave their homelands for a variety of reasons, yet political and economic circumstances are perhaps the most common. Many students have left loved ones behind, along with a familiar and cherished way of life. For some, it is the dream and expectation that they will return to their country when a war is ended or when the family has enough money to better their lives in their home country. These students may not feel a great need to become proficient in a language they don't intend to use for very long.

- **Poverty.** Living in poverty and experiencing food insecurity has a profound impact on learning in general, and that extends to learning a language. Simply said, when poverty is addressed so that students' basic needs are met, they are more likely to excel in school.

- **Personality.** Some students are naturally outgoing and verbal; others are shy or prefer more independent activities. Some are risk takers who are not afraid to make mistakes; others want their utterances to be perfect. These personality differences can lead to differences in the rate at which students gain proficiency in listening and speaking or reading and writing.

Marking the Development of Multilingual Learners

Multilingual learners progress through stages as they reach increasing proficiency. Typically, proficiency starts with a silent phase in which the student does very little talking (Lai & Wang, 2016). We've all seen a student who seems reserved but is taking in everything. In all likelihood, if this student is an emergent multilingual learner, they are assimilating the sounds of English and learning basic vocabulary.

As an example, consider Sari, a wide-eyed and inquisitive student who emigrated from Cambodia and participated in her district's newcomer program. With support and a risk-free environment, Sari started talking in a matter of a few months, positioning herself well on her way to academic success and English proficiency. In this case, the respectful treatment of her silent period, which gave her the time to become more comfortable with her early attempts, was critical for her language development.

As students like Sari develop language, they move through a continuum of increasing skill and understanding. California's proficiency levels identify three language proficiency levels that are used for instructional purposes: *emerging, expanding,* and *bridging.* Most states have developed sets of standards for proficiency levels or use those developed by WIDA (https://wida.wisc.edu/resources/performance-definitions-expressive-domains), though they may call them by other names. Figure 1.1 features a list of performance definitions used by California to describe each level.

FIGURE 1.1	California Performance Definitions for Three Levels of English Language Proficiency

English language learners can understand and use . . .	
Level 1 Emerging	Students at this level typically progress quickly, learn to use English for immediate needs, and begin to understand and use academic language for the grade level, with substantial language support provided.
Level 2 Expanding	Students at this level use their growing language skills in more advanced ways that are appropriate to their age and grade level, with moderate language support provided.
Level 3 Bridging	Students at this level can independently use a variety of high-level English language skills and fully participate in grade-level academic activities in all content areas, with light language support provided.

Source: Adapted from Sacramento County Office of Education (n.d.).

Conclusion

The reality is that multilingual learners must make significant progress each year to catch up to a moving target. Some students do not make that much progress, especially when teachers' expectations are low or there is faulty or infrequent communication with families. Educators must examine the learning conditions that are needed in the classroom to promote learning. As educators, we must remember that our students bring a wealth of background knowledge and experiences that can support learning new content in a new language, but they may need guidance in making those connections and drawing upon their prior knowledge. We can ensure that multilingual learners succeed by focusing on the classroom learning environment we create.

Climate for Learning

2

Big Idea

Multilingual learners thrive when the classroom climate supports their needs, including belonging and understanding how the environment operates.

Questions Educators Ask

- How can I foster a sense of belonging in the classroom?

- What role should peers play in the learning of others?

- How might the classroom be organized to support learning, and what agreements do we need to have as a class?

- How does grouping students contribute to a thriving learning environment?

Ask any educator about the foundations of learning, and they will inevitably speak about the importance of the classroom learning environment. Not surprisingly, the effect size numbers (www.visiblelearn ingmetax.com) really back this up:

- Relationships between teacher and students (effect size of 0.47)
- Proactive classroom management (effect size of 0.35)
- Friendships (effect size of 0.29)
- Feeling a sense of belonging (effect size of 0.40)

Not only do these incredible numbers hover right around the average for *all influences on learning,* but they also represent some necessary conditions for learning. In fact, when these conditions are not present, tremendous damage can be done. For example, the effect size of feeling disliked by the teacher and peers is −0.26, being bullied is −0.33, and feeling bored due to a disconnection from the content and instruction is −0.33.

The classroom environment, first and foremost, either cultivates or inhibits the social, emotional, psychological, and motivational dimensions of learning that are essential for all students to thrive. These messages are conveyed through the relational and physical attributes of the room. An important outcome of these influences is the perception that the adult(s) in the room and the students are all on the same page, an element referred to as *classroom cohesion.* Classroom cohesion consists of "positive interpersonal relations between students, a sense of belonging of all students, and group solidarity" (Veerman & Denessen, 2021).

> The classroom environment either cultivates or inhibits the dimensions of learning that are essential for all students to thrive.

Belonging

Maslow's hierarchy of needs is well known among educators, but its roots may not be. In 1943, Maslow wrote an article titled "A Theory of Human Motivation." Maslow believed it is necessary to *motivate* humans to develop and grow to achieve their individual potential (see Figure 2.1). Belonging, he posited, is an essential dimension for unlocking motivation.

In the article, Maslow explained that basic physiological and psychological needs are crucial. A child who is underfed or fearful is not likely to be motivated to learn. But as you review Figure 2.1, note that belonging is the next step. Also notice what it precedes: achievement and mastery. When students don't feel like they belong, achievement—learning—is not going to happen. Yet too often classrooms are structured such that achievement is how students gain belonging. The underlying message these classrooms send is this: "Because you achieve, you belong." Think how wrongheaded that is. How do we create a classroom where our multilingual learners have a sense of belonging in place (or the support they need to form one) so they can proceed to the next steps and achieve?

FIGURE 2.1   Maslow's Hierarchy of Needs

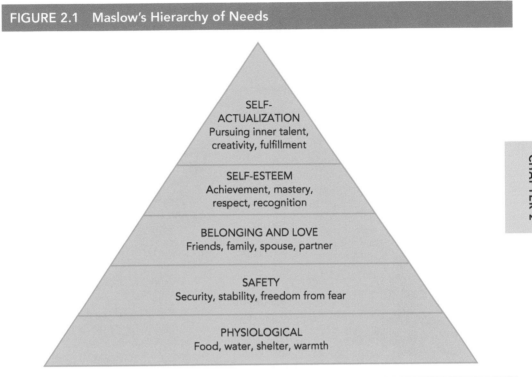

Source: **Maslow (1943).**

Multilingual learners face various obstacles when they arrive at a new classroom or school. As new members of the community, they may find themselves on the outside looking in. Yet they are seeking to fit in, to find a group to belong to, a tribe they can call their own. A classroom that celebrates students' different values, beliefs, cultures, and languages can foster belonging, which contributes positively to strong classroom cohesion. When students sense that their individual experiences are respected and valued, they also feel like they belong.

Along these lines, Carter (2021) argues that educators need to create a sense of belonging in classrooms and schools. Carter notes that students experience belonging when they are "present, invited, welcomed, known, accepted, supported, heard, befriended, needed, and loved" (p. 16). Each of these factors can impact multilingual learners and their belief that

When students sense that their individual experiences are respected and valued, they also feel like they belong.

they belong in the school. Carter offers some questions, which we have adapted to support multilingual learners, for educators to reflect on:

- **Present:** Is our community comprised of individuals whose languages, experiences, and backgrounds vary?

- **Invited:** Are we pursuing multilingual learners' presence and actively extending new invitations?

- **Welcomed:** Are we extending a warm welcome whenever multilingual learners arrive?

- **Known:** Do we know multilingual learners personally and for the strengths they possess?

- **Accepted:** Are we receiving multilingual learners unconditionally and graciously?

- **Heard:** Are we seeking out multilingual learners' preferences and perspectives on issues that matter?

- **Supported:** Are we providing the assistance multilingual learners need to participate fully and meaningfully?

- **Befriended:** Are we creating opportunities for friendships to form and deepen between all our students?

- **Needed:** Are we recognizing and receiving our multilingual learners' talents, gifts, and contributions?

- **Loved:** Are we loving our multilingual learners deeply and unconditionally?

As Carter and Biggs (2021) note, "We all hope that students will feel truly 'at home' in their classrooms. We want them to feel valued and accepted by their peers and teachers. We strive to create connections among students that lead to reciprocal relationships." That's a good place to start when it comes to creating the climate for learning that multilingual learners need. As part of this climate, educators can create an environment that includes an ethical imperative—to teach and support others when we learn something.

Peers Helping Peers

The cohesion of the class is fostered further by expectations about how students take care of one another. One way of crafting such a message is through the helping curriculum, a term coined by Sapon-Shevin (1998). The helping curriculum consists of four expectations:

- I offer help.

- I accept help.

- I ask for help.

- I politely decline help when I want to continue trying on my own.

Embedded in the helping curriculum are two influences that have the potential to accelerate learning: help seeking and persistence. Help seeking is associated with higher levels of achievement (effect size of 0.85). Persistence, which is a dimension of effort management, has an effect size of 0.51 (www.visiblelearningmetax.com). Both influences reflect a common strength: self-regulation. Help seeking requires self-awareness of the need for assistance, possessing techniques for requesting it, and making strategic decisions about whom to ask. Effort management requires that students know how to manage their mood, engage in self-talk, and attribute their success to effort, which is often called a *growth mindset* (Dweck, 2006).

One technique often used to support emergent multilingual learners is to pair them with another student who speaks the same heritage language but has a higher degree of proficiency in English. Defining the purpose of the "buddy" work based on the desired outcome can make peer relationships far more effective so that the same students are not always tapped to serve in the support role. Figure 2.2 illustrates how educators can match the purpose to the choice of partners.

CHAPTER 2

Embedded in the helping curriculum are two influences that have the potential to accelerate learning: help seeking and persistence.

FIGURE 2.2   Pairings in the Helping Curriculum

IF THE DESIRED OUTCOME IS TO HELP THE MULTILINGUAL STUDENT DO THE FOLLOWING . . .	THEN EDUCATORS SHOULD PAIR THE STUDENT* WITH A "BUDDY" WHO . . .
Adjust to their new environment	Speaks the same language or has a similar background
Use more English	Speaks English and is patient
Learn from peers	Enjoys teaching others and is helpful
Help peers	Speaks the same language and can benefit from the partnership
Develop persistence	Knows how to offer encouragement
Become part of the learning community	Is outgoing and connected with other students

*Educators should change these partners often to encourage relationships.

Setting the Physical Environment

Spaces speak to people and send messages about how they should act in the setting. For example, the high ceilings of a place of worship remind congregants how small they are and signal that they should use quiet voices. A crowded and narrow street provokes a heightened sense of awareness for many people, and perhaps some anxiety.

Similarly, classroom design conveys messages about what is valued and who is valued. Often without realizing it, students make several judgments about the teacher and about themselves based on the physical environment. They analyze elements and reach conclusions such as the following:

- Is it organized and neat? So is my teacher.

- Are there interesting items on display for me to use? This is my classroom and I belong here.

- Are there indicators that I am not welcome here? Signs such as "keep out" or "not for student use" can convey an unwelcoming environment and can be rephrased.

> Classroom
> design
> conveys
> messages
> about what
> is valued and
> who is valued.

Lots of clutter can provoke anxiety in some students. It can also tell a tale of disarray rather than convey the teacher's anticipation of the students' presence. Neon colors, often popular in elementary classrooms, can actually trigger negative physiological responses, such as more rapid breathing and heart rate (Elliott et al., 2015).

Emmer et al. (2002) advise teachers to consider visibility, proximity, and accessibility when arranging a classroom. Because each classroom is unique, the arrangement you decide on will be influenced by your academic needs and by student considerations. Keep in mind that multilingual students may have learning needs that require particular classroom placement to increase visibility or minimize distractions. They may rely heavily on the nonlinguistic signals that your room arrangement conveys.

Students need to be able to hear, see, and move around the classroom in order to engage in the learning opportunities you are offering. If you fail to attend to these issues, the classroom limitations can result in learning difficulties for individual students. In particular, when the room's physical messages are confusing or contradictory, multilingual students may misinterpret them. Then you may misinterpret the students' behavior as problematic when it's really the product of confusion.

In addition, your own activity in the classroom must also be factored in as you consider the general setup. You need to be able to easily access materials, work with individual students, engage in small-group discussions, and display information. Use the following set of guiding questions to develop a room arrangement that works well for you and your students.

- **Visibility.** Are there areas of the classroom where students cannot easily view the board or screen? If so, consider using these areas for other purposes, including small-group work or storage.

- **Proximity.** Proximity is the physical distance between you and a student, and it is a useful tool for increasing student engagement. Look at the pathways for teacher movement in your classroom. Can you easily reach each student in the room to provide extra instructional or behavioral support? Can you circulate during whole-group teaching to monitor learning? Keep proximity between students in mind as well. Engaging classrooms use partner arrangements throughout the day. Be certain that students can easily move into partner groups at your direction.

- **Accessibility.** An orderly learning environment allows students to reach materials and areas of the classroom easily. Students need to sharpen pencils, retrieve laptops, throw away trash, enter and exit the room, and choose books from the classroom library. When planning your room arrangement, consider patterns of movement in these high-traffic areas.

Students need to be able to hear, see, and move around the classroom in order to engage in the learning opportunities you are offering.

The Reggio Emilia Approach is a method used in preschool and primary classrooms worldwide. Its philosophy is built on the idea that three teachers inform the child: the educator, the child's family, and the environment. Even if you don't teach very young children, you can appreciate the notion that the spatial environment signals to your students how learning occurs. Use the questions in Figure 2.3, adapted from the Australia Children's Education and Care Quality Authority, to assess how your classroom conveys an inviting message for learning (Fisher & Frey, 2022).

FIGURE 2.3 Learning Environment Survey

LEARNING ENVIRONMENT CRITERIA	MY EVIDENCE
1. How does this classroom encourage students to make choices and learn decision making?	
2. How does this classroom support students' sense of security?	
3. Is there evidence of displays of student work, and what role do students have in selecting work for display?	
4. How are displays of student work a reflection of works in progress, not just final versions?	
5. How does this classroom encourage collaboration among students?	
6. How do classroom materials reflect the interests, experiences, and cultures of students and the community?	

Source: Adapted from Australia Children's Education and Care Quality Authority (2018).

Classroom Agreements

In addition to the physical dimension of the classroom, the social dynamics are crucial and deserve attention. Most teachers have classroom rules or classroom agreements that are meant to shape the norms of how everyone works, resolves problems, and engages with others. Classroom rules, which should be co-constructed by the teacher and the students, are "statements that teachers present to describe acceptable and unacceptable behavior" (Alter & Haydon, 2017, p. 115). The authors systematically reviewed the literature on these practices. Using the findings from fifteen studies, they identified the following themes:

- Keep the number between three and six statements.

- Create them collaboratively with students.

- State them positively.

- Word them specifically so that students understand them.

- Publicly post them.

- Teach them and refer to them often.

- Link them to positive and negative consequences.

The dialogic nature of classroom shared agreements that are co-developed offers an opportunity for you to highlight the social and emotional learning that is needed for multilingual students to succeed. The Collaborative for Academic, Social, and Emotional Learning (CASEL) publishes a tool for generating classroom shared agreements that can be downloaded (CASEL, 2019; https://schoolguide.casel .org/resource/sample-lesson-plan-generating-classroom-shared-agreements). We have highlighted the sequence of discussions here (CASEL, 2019):

1. Introduce shared classroom agreements and discuss their purpose (e.g., What does it mean to have a safe classroom? Why is it important to create a classroom where everyone feels physically and emotionally safe?).

2. Discuss how the students want to be treated by others and how they might treat others this year.

3. Brainstorm ideas for classroom shared agreements. Record students' ideas for how they will treat others this year, using their own words. Group ideas that capture what they have identified.

4. After the lesson, make a large poster of the shared agreements, leaving room for each student to sign.

5. Review the classroom shared agreements on a regular basis and integrate them into your daily routines.

We also recommend using these as a platform for backward planning. Once the shared agreements have been established, discuss how these agreements are manifested. In other words, how do they look and sound in action?

Let's look at one example of a common problem that may arise for multilingual learners: teasing, name calling, and bullying. Teasing, name calling, and exclusion are the most common forms of verbal and relational aggression for multilingual students, and they include attacks on identity, ethnicity, race, and language (Pratt-Johnson, 2015). In addition, some multilingual learners may lack the language skills in English to prevent or stop a bullying incident (Ostrander et al., 2018). Despite the acknowledgment that bias about language skills is a form of bullying, many adults consider it a normal—even necessary—part of childhood. However, bullying can undermine the classroom community and is perceived as acceptable when the teacher does little to respond to it. Here's how teachers can work with students to proactively head off conflicts and help resolve them when they occur.

Establish a Classroom Rule
Aligned to the Shared Agreement

The playground is the harshest environment for some children, especially those seen as outsiders by others. Left unchecked, some children may exclude one another from play, often hurling uncharitable words in the process. A shared agreement with the class might be something like, "We will take care of each other." But how is that expressed in daily classroom interactions? Fine-tuning the rule authored in partnership with the class can eliminate such interactions.

For example, this revised or added rule may be worded as "Everyone here can play" (Paley, 1992). The intent of this rule is to eliminate exclusion by requiring students to create a way for a classmate to join a group at play. This should help prevent them from simply telling the child, "You can't play with us." Once a rule is established, children will need many opportunities to practice using it. You should model this behavior as the teacher and praise the students when you witness it.

Create a Forum for Students to Resolve Disputes With Your Assistance

Even with a proactive approach, bullying issues can still arise. Again, the eyes of your students are on you. View this as an opportunity to teach, not just as a problem to solve. All students should be taught how to resolve disputes when they arise. These steps can serve children well when an argument flares up. The establishment of a peace table can provide children with both the space and the structure to resolve problems in a constructive manner. Here's what this might look like in practice.

- **Meet with both parties separately.** There are issues to address on both sides. Each student needs to hear directly from you about the problem and the solution. Help prepare each party for the facilitated discussion that will follow:

  1. Help students to develop an "I" statement to explain how they are feeling. ("When you _____ I felt _____. I would like for you to _____.")

  2. Teach them to listen to what the other child has to say.

  3. Remind them to discuss the problem calmly until they arrive at a solution both of them can agree upon.

- **Mediate the discussion at the peace table**. The peace table should be situated in a quiet spot in the room or elsewhere in the school for students to discuss their dispute with some privacy. Ask the students to take ownership of their behavior and broker apologies, solutions, and future promises as needed.

- **Notify the families so they can collaborate with you.** Don't hesitate to consult with the families to solve the problem. They often source the best ideas for working effectively with their child.

- **Get the school administration involved.** Incidents of bullying can rapidly spiral into serious situations. Make sure an administrator and counselor are involved in solving bullying problems that do not respond to classroom interventions.

Grouping Students

Classrooms that provide maximum opportunities for students to talk are organized around a variety of grouping configurations. Students frequently work collaboratively with others, in pairs or small groups, to develop skills, complete a task, and construct meaning.

Classrooms that provide maximum opportunities for students to talk are organized around a variety of grouping configurations.

The ways you group students for teacher-directed instruction and peer-to-peer collaborative learning actually influence what they learn (or do not learn). In part, this is because your grouping decisions reflect your expectations for students.

Researchers followed the mathematics progress of nearly more than three thousand kindergarten multilingual learners and compared them to their teachers' expectations and grouping practices (Garrett & Hong, 2016). Their results linked the relative achievement of students to two factors: grouping and teacher expectations. Teachers with lower expectations for students relied more on whole-group instruction and homogeneous small groups that were based on language proficiency. Teachers with higher expectations used a combination of heterogeneous and homogeneous small-group instruction and less whole-group instruction. In addition, these teachers formatively assessed more often than those with lower expectations for students.

Students who are not yet making expected progress are vulnerable to the grouping practices of teachers. Those who are in classrooms that use whole-group instruction are less likely to be assessed formatively, and therefore they are less likely to have instruction adjusted to meet their needs. In addition, low-achieving students in peer-led homogeneous groups are more likely to languish because they lack the collective academic, language, and social resources necessary to progress. When it comes to students of concern, grouping can make a difference in students' learning.

Student grouping should be intentional, assessment driven, and flexible.

Effective small-group heterogeneous grouping (groups that do not remain permanent, change a lot, and capitalize on the variance in the group) involves more than randomly assigning students to groups and hoping for the best. Student grouping should be intentional, assessment driven, and flexible. This is crucial for students who are not yet making expected progress, as the ratio of higher- and lower-achieving students within the small group can play a factor. For example, the needs of a single lower-achieving student in the presence of too many high-achieving peers can mean that student's voice is drowned out as others dominate.

Another consideration is the relative range within a group. A wide academic or linguistic gap between students can pose a communication challenge that learners may not know how to bridge. In both cases, there is an increased likelihood that some students will dominate the task while others are left to (or choose to) passively observe.

One method for constructing sound heterogeneous small groups is to use an alternate ranking system. Here's how that works:

1. Use a recent assessment formatively to rank students in order from highest to lowest achieving on a recent assessment.

2. Split the list in half to form two sub-lists. In a class of 32, Sublist A lists students 1–16, while Sublist B lists students 17–32.

3. Use the top two names from Sublist A and the top two names from Sublist B to form a group of four students. Thus, students 1, 2, 17, and 18 are a heterogeneous group.

4. Repeat this to form a group composed of students 3, 4, 19, and 20.

5. Continue this process until all students are grouped. In this case, the final group would consist of students 15, 16, 31, and 32 (see Figure 2.4).

FIGURE 2.4   Alternate Ranking Example

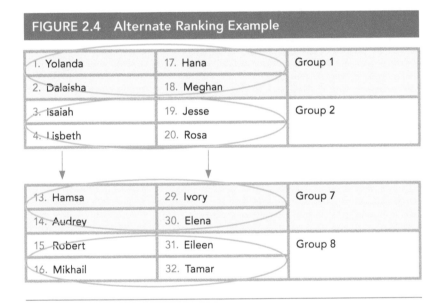

Alternate ranking simultaneously accomplishes two purposes. It maintains heterogeneity across groups, while it also brackets the relative range of cognitive, social, and language resources within. Of course, this approach isn't foolproof. Be sure to use your own knowledge of your students to make any necessary adjustments.

The way that students are grouped sends powerful messages about who is, and who is not, valued in the classroom. Students notice if they are always placed in the same groups, and their peers notice who is allowed to work with whom. Ineffective grouping impacts learning opportunities as well as changes the social dynamics of the classroom.

Conclusion

There is always a climate in the classroom. Students are much more likely to learn when it is nurtured and supported. When it is ignored or neglected, the climate can become toxic for some—or even all—of the students, and it can compromise their learning. Of course, there is more to learning for multilingual learners than a supportive climate, but creating a sense of belonging, peer supports, and agreement about how things happen sets the stage for learning to occur.

Challenge as Learning

3

//

Big Idea

Multilingual learners want to be challenged, and they want their teachers to believe that they can learn at high levels by assigning them tasks that are rigorous.

Questions Educators Ask

- What actions convey high expectations?

- How can tasks be designed to balance difficulty and complexity?

- How can students be supported to develop persistence and resilience when they struggle?

Students want learning to be a challenge. They are not interested in boring tasks and busy work. In a survey of 452,329 students, 83 percent of the respondents said that they push themselves to do better academically, and 42 percent said they liked challenging assignments (Quaglia Institute, 2022). Unfortunately, most of the assignments given to students are well below grade level. As noted by TNTP (2018), based on their review of more than 20,000 assignments, students spent, on average, 133 out of every 180 hours—73 percent of their time—on below-grade-level tasks. This report also noted that in four out of every ten classrooms with a majority of students of color, students never received a single grade-level assignment.

However, their 2022 report notes that students generally get the same number of questions correct irrespective of the level of rigor. Over the course of ten assignments, students answered 68 percent of the questions correctly on below-grade-level assignments and 63 percent of the questions correctly on grade-level assignments. Are three additional questions answered correctly by students over the course of ten assignments really worth lowering expectations for them? What might change for our students if we actually expect them to perform academically at high levels?

We noted the value of teacher expectations in Chapter 1. We introduced the New Zealand researcher Rubie-Davis who has shown that teachers with high expectations tend to have them for all students. In contrast, sadly, teachers with low expectations tend to have them for all students. And both are successful at either raising (an effect size of 0.90) or lowering progress and attainment (the effect size is 0.06) for their students.

Teacher perceptions and expectations can become students' realities. Several decades ago, Good (1987) published his review of twenty years of evidence on teacher expectations. He noted significant differences in how teachers treated students they believed were low achieving. Good found that low-achieving students

- Are criticized more often for failure
- Are praised less frequently
- Receive less feedback
- Are called on less often
- Have less eye contact with the teacher
- Have fewer friendly interactions with the teacher
- Experience acceptance of their ideas less often

There is another term for this: a "chilly" classroom climate in which some students do not feel they are valued and instead feel that "their presence . . . is at best peripheral, and at worst an unwelcome intrusion" (Hall & Sandler, 1982, p. 3).

We do not in any way believe that these differential teacher behaviors are conscious and intentional. One speculation is that we subconsciously avoid contact with them because educators don't feel successful with students they view as lower achieving. After all, teachers were human beings long before they became educators, and as social animals, humans attempt to surround themselves with people who make them feel good about themselves. Teachers who work with students who are

CHAPTER 3

What might change for our students if we actually expect them to perform academically at high levels?

not making gains can begin to feel like failures, and so they detach themselves even more.

Using Good's research, we created the tool in Figure 3.1 for you to use to assess you and your colleagues might differentially interact with students. Remember, these are subconscious and unconscious behaviors. But more importantly, they can be changed through intentional actions. Our goal is to help teachers notice, and then change, their interactions with students and increase their expectations. For each of the items identified in Figure 3.1, consider three students who are not currently performing well in your class. Then decide if you can re-recruit them into learning by changing some of these interaction patterns.

FIGURE 3.1   Interactions That Invite Students Into Learning

INTERACTION	STUDENT 1	STUDENT 2	STUDENT 3
Did you greet the student by name when they entered the classroom?			
How many times did you use their name (not as a correction) during the class?			
Did you ask them a critical-thinking question related to the content?			
Did you ask them a personal question?			
Did you group the student by a perceived ability?			
Did you pay them a compliment?			
How many times did you provide them with praise for their learning performance?			

Teachers with high expectations believe that their students will make accelerated growth, not simply "normal" progress (Rubie-Davies, 2014). Teachers with lower expectations assign tasks that are less cognitively demanding, spend time repeating information over and over again, focus on classroom rules and procedures, and accept a lower standard of work (Rubie-Davies, 2008). As summarized by the Education Hub (2018), high-expectation teachers do the following:

- Communicate learning intentions and success criteria with the class.

- Ask more open questions, designed to extend or enhance students' thinking by requiring them to think more deeply.

- Manage behavior positively and proactively.

- Make more positive statements and create a positive class climate.

- Set specific goals with students that are regularly reviewed and used for teaching and learning.

- Take a facilitative role and support students to make choices about their learning.

- Link achievement to motivation, effort, and goal setting.

- Encourage students to work with a variety of peers for positive peer modeling.

- Provide less differentiation and allow all learners to engage in advanced activities.

- Undertake more assessment and monitoring so that students' learning strategies can be adjusted when necessary.

- Work with all students equally.

- Give specific, instructional feedback about students' achievement in relation to learning goals.

- Respond to incorrect answers by exploring the wrong answer, rephrasing explanations, or scaffolding the student to the correct answer.

- Base learning opportunities around students' interests for motivation. (p. 4)

Use the self-assessment checklist in Figure 3.2 to identify the frequency of the high-expectation practices that you use.

FIGURE 3.2   High-Expectation Practices

HOW OFTEN DO YOU USE THE FOLLOWING HIGH-EXPECTATION PRACTICES IN YOUR TEACHING?	RARELY	SOMETIMES	OFTEN
Ask open questions			
Praise effort rather than correct answers			
Use regular formative assessment			
Rephrase questions when answers are incorrect			

HOW OFTEN DO YOU USE THE FOLLOWING HIGH-EXPECTATION PRACTICES IN YOUR TEACHING?	RARELY	SOMETIMES	OFTEN
Use mixed-ability groupings			
Change groupings regularly			
Encourage students to work with a range of their peers			
Provide a range of activities			
Allow students to choose their own activities from a range of options			
Make explicit learning intentions and success criteria			
Allow students to contribute to success criteria			
Give students responsibility for their learning			
Get to know each student personally			
Incorporate students' interests into activities			
Establish routines and procedures at the beginning of the school year			
Work with students to set individual goals			
Teach students about SMART (specific, measurable, achievable, relevant, and time-bound) goals			
Regularly review goals with students			
Link achievement to motivation, effort, and goal setting			
Minimize differentiation in activities between high and low achievers			
Allow all learners to engage in advanced activities			
Give specific, instructional feedback about students' achievement in relation to learning goals			
Take a facilitative role and support students to make choices about their learning			
Manage behavior positively and proactively			
Work with all students equally			

Source: The Education Hub (2018).

Designing Complex Tasks

We like to think of *difficulty* as the amount of effort, time, or work a student is expected to put forth; *complexity* is the level of thinking, the number of steps, or the abstractness of the task.

In attempts to raise the rigor of student tasks and assignments, teachers cannot simply make them more difficult. Instead, teachers need to consider the complexity of these tasks and assignments. We like to think of *difficulty* as the amount of effort, time, or work a student is expected to put forth, whereas *complexity* is the level of thinking, the number of steps, or the abstractness of the task. We don't believe teachers can radically impact student learning by simply assigning more and more work. The type of work and the complexity of that work make a difference. We know that students learn more when they are engaged in deeper thinking. We know that students learn more when they are engaged in deeper thinking.

That's not to say that difficulty is bad. We think of this in four quadrants (see Figure 3.3). The quadrant that includes low difficulty and low complexity is not unimportant. (We believe note taking fits into that quadrant.) If all the tasks students experience in the classroom fall in the fourth quadrant, then learning isn't likely to be robust. As part of each lesson, teachers should know the level of difficulty and complexity they are requiring of students.

FIGURE 3.3   Comparing Difficulty and Complexity

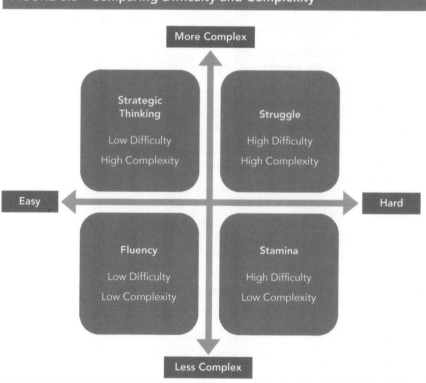

Some tasks require a lot of effort, such as writing a research paper. If you've never done it before, it will take some organizing. It is also complex because of the materials you need to assemble and use, decisions about the order to perform each of the steps, and so on. But if you've done this a lot of times, while the effort may still be considerable, the complexity decreases because you have refined your writing procedures. The tasks we design for our students should balance difficulty and complexity. We need our students to engage with all four quadrants if they are to experience rigorous learning. Let's consider each of these and the types of tasks appropriate for multilingual learners.

The tasks we design for our students should balance difficulty and complexity.

Fluency

In the lower left-hand quadrant, tasks are low difficulty and low complexity. We think of this as the *fluency* quadrant, as in procedural and conceptual fluency. More formally, this would be called *automaticity,* the goal of all instructional efforts. Over time, and with practice, skills should become automatic for students.

When students reach automaticity, they no longer use their working memory to accomplish tasks. Instead, their working memory is freed to focus on problem solving and reflection. For example, this happens with decoding, number sense, using information from the periodic table of elements, and corroborating information within an informational text.

Note that fluency is not simply about basic skills, but any process we practice sufficiently to create a habit. In terms of instruction for multilingual learners, there may be skills that English-proficient students have that multilingual learners still need to develop. And it's important to remember that all students need practice to maintain their fluency. Consequently, lessons should include opportunities to practice, or even over-practice, to ensure learning (e.g., Anderson et al., 1999).

Stamina

In the bottom lower-right quadrant, difficulty has increased but complexity remains low. We think of this as the *stamina* quadrant. Tasks in this quadrant require perseverance, determination, and grit. Students must remain focused and work to complete these types of tasks, which require their ability to work independently versus giving up when the going gets tough.

Students need to experience tasks that require their stamina, and they need to hear from valued adults that their efforts are worthy, valuable, and noticed. For multilingual learners, it can be very frustrating and exhausting to work in a new language for long periods of time. In

CHAPTER 3

addition to building stamina, multilingual learners need an opportunity to communicate in their home languages or through multiple modalities. Thus, teachers need to parse tasks and set goals that slowly and surely increase students' stamina. For example, we know that wide reading builds vocabulary and background knowledge, but students may not be reading for twenty or more minutes each day after school. In this case, setting goals that increase stamina can help students eventually accomplish more reading. The same is true with other tasks that require stamina, such as rich mathematics and science investigations.

Students can often complete tasks that fall below the horizontal (easy to hard) line individually and independently. Teachers and parents can create tasks, assignments, and activities for students to do by themselves that build their fluency and stamina. For example, sight word recognition is a fluency activity. One of our friends has a young child who wanted to learn to read. To help him, she listed more than one hundred sight words on index cards. As he read them, he got to keep the cards he knew, while she kept the cards he did not yet know. Over the course of a couple of months, he mastered all the cards, and he still likes to play the game to show that he can win all the cards. Our friend has continued to add new words to the stack as his reading skills progress. Of course, there is much more to reading, but sight word recognition is an important aspect and a task that requires stamina.

Strategic Thinking

The upper left-hand quadrant, in which complexity increases but difficulty does not, requires that students engage in *strategic thinking*. Strategic thinking has been defined in various ways, but it includes the following abilities:

- Formulate goals and create a plan to achieve them.
- Gather and integrate information.
- Make decisions about how to proceed.
- Reflect on one's actions and thinking.
- Adjust actions based on these reflections.

To engage in strategic thinking, students must slow down and focus. Even though there may not be much difficulty, the task is complex. There's a name for this—*cognitive task analysis*—and the effect size is 1.29. Cognitive task analysis involves successfully analyzing the steps required to complete a cognitive task. It involves knowing the surface, deep, and transfer knowledge, and the learning strategies required for success at each level. For example, while reading a dense piece of informational text in social studies, students may realize that the author has provided a great deal of information and that they should take notes for later. That's a strategic thought.

Similarly, when the teacher assigns a multistep, extended project, students should learn to ask themselves if they are on the right track, if their efforts meet the success criteria, if they are likely to meet the deadline, and if each member of the group has an opportunity to contribute. These are also strategic thoughts. Finally, when students learn to infer, set goals for themselves, plan their studying, and monitor their comprehension, they are engaged in strategic thinking. It's important to also recognize that when students receive feedback on their strategic-thinking efforts and see others engage in strategic thinking, these actions begin to become habits or fluent behaviors.

Struggle

We think of the final quadrant, the upper right side, as the *struggle* quadrant. Tasks in this quadrant are complex and difficult. They are time-consuming and require deeper thinking. We named this quadrant *struggle* to encourage teachers to design experiences for students that required learners to grapple with ideas, information, concepts, and skills. For example, when students read multiple documents in a science class and then have to present their findings, they are likely engaged in a task that requires expertise. These tasks demand mastery of basic skills and competency in content knowledge.

Students are expected to apply their knowledge and skills in unique ways to solve complex problems in this quadrant. As an example, rich mathematical tasks usually fall into this quadrant. These tasks typically have multiple ways to reach a solution, require trial and error, and have the potential to reveal patterns or lead to generalizations or unexpected results. They are not easy to solve but are interesting, and students tend to find them worth their time. Having said that, we do not expect that classroom lessons are limited to tasks that require struggle. All four quadrants are important and contribute to the learning and development of students.

Unfortunately, students who are not yet making expected progress are frequently relegated to tasks below the line (fluency and stamina), with fewer opportunities to engage in strategic thinking and problem solving. The result is that learning is inhibited, and they continue to fail to make progress. Rigor means that we challenge all of our students and include opportunities for them to struggle. In terms of the effect on learning, Hattie terms this the Goldilocks level of challenge: not too hard and not

When students learn to infer, set goals for themselves, plan their studying, and monitor their comprehension, they are engaged in strategic thinking.

CHAPTER 3

too boring. When teachers accomplish this, students learn more, and the effect size is 0.74: above average in the potential to accelerate learning.

Persistence and Resilience

Rigor means that we challenge all of our students and include opportunities for them to struggle.

Persistence is the ability to continue in the face of adversity and setbacks, while resilience is the ability to recover from and adapt to challenging circumstances. As adults who have acquired a bit of life experience, we can all appreciate the need for persistence to achieve a long-term goal, paired with an aptitude for meeting challenges without being defeated by them. For students, these character traits are positively correlated and predictive of school enjoyment, class participation, and self-esteem (Martin & Marsh, 2006). It's also effective for learning, with persistence having an effect size of 0.51. One group of researchers (Morell et al., 2021) found that perseverance of effort (perseverance in working toward goals) predicted student grades more than the consistency of effort (pursuit of a goal with passion).

As teachers, we are charged with more than monitoring students' immediate success. What level of persistence do they display? Along those lines, the second characteristic—resilience—involves more than just being able to bounce back when something negative occurs. Duckworth, who studies grit, says that resiliency is also about "optimism—appraising situations without distorting them, thinking about changes that are possible to make in your life" (Perkins-Gough & Duckworth, 2013, p. 14). Classrooms have the potential for building resilience and encouraging persistence.

Use Language That Encourages Persistence

By using language that builds agency and identity, we can help students recognize what they are capable of doing. By eliminating general statements such as "You're such a great writer" and replacing them with specific praise like "Your writing is great because you've put the time and effort into polishing this," we remind learners that it's effort, not latent talent, that makes a difference. To be clear, this is not about telling students they are wonderful no matter what; it's about providing positive feedback and actionable steps they can take to continue learning.

Along these lines, adults should engage with students who are feeling paralyzed by indecision and assist them with formulating a plan for addressing the dilemma. For instance, one day a ninth-grade student told Nancy that she didn't know how she was going to finish an essay, so Nancy helped her devise a plan for what she would do for the final thirty minutes of class. Here's what this looked like in practice.

CHAPTER 3

First, Nancy validated the student's experience. She said, "Thinking about the whole task can be overwhelming, I agree."

Then she helped the student move forward, by prompting, "Let's think about the next right thing to do."

The student then explained that she was most distressed about the errors in her work. Together they located the MLA style handbook, which was posted on the learning management system, and the student corrected the references before the end of class.

Next, Nancy spoke with her again, this time about what she had accomplished and what she would do that evening. In helping the student develop a plan, Nancy reinforced a mindset about the benefit that comes from effort and persistence.

Researchers who study persistence note that there are several things that teachers can do to help students develop stamina (e.g., Duckworth, 2016; Tough, 2012). Let's take a quick look.

Help Learners Understand and Develop a Growth Mindset Way of Thinking

Dweck (2006) suggested growth mindsets can inspire different goals and shape views about effort, but she did not suggest that there was a state of mind called a *growth mindset*. It's not a mindset or attribution of a person, but rather a way of thinking in particular situations (Hattie, 2017). The critical situation is when the student is confused, not knowing, making errors, or anxious. For example, students who see failure as debilitating and reflective of their abilities, rather than as an opportunity to learn something new, need guidance in thinking differently. But this way of thinking is not just about building confidence. In fact, when students are overconfident, they allocate less time to difficult problems (Dweck, 2016). Thinking in a growth manner versus in a fixed manner is especially useful in these situations:

- When we do not know an answer
- When we make an error
- When we experience failure
- When we are anxious

Having a growth mindset is a most appropriate coping strategy, and it needs to be taught and acknowledged within school subjects (not in separate growth classes). In essence, educators need to help students

By using language that builds agency and identity, we can help students recognize what they are capable of doing.

CHAPTER 3

understand that their intelligence or abilities can be changed and that it is not fixed and immutable.

Push, but Know When to Stop

The expectations must be clear, and when students want to quit, they need firm and gentle support from another person to keep going. Teachers should avoid telling students answers when they are wrong or when they are stuck. Rather, teachers should prompt and cue students toward the correct information. Importantly, students persist longer for teachers with whom they have great relationships. As Honigsfeld et al. (2021) remind us, teachers of multilingual learners need to harness the power of connections and relationships.

Students don't want to disappoint the teachers they care about, so they keep trying, often learning more in the process. As we will see later in this book, effective teachers use a gradual release of responsibility framework to support students' learning, assuming increased responsibilities at some points in the lesson and releasing responsibility at other points.

Model Perseverance

Far too many students lack an example of persistence. In fact, many students believe that learning comes easy for their teachers, and some think that their teachers already know everything. Young people need to see the adults in their lives persevere. They appreciate knowing that their teachers try, sometimes fail, and then try again. When we think aloud and show students that we get stuck and have to resolve issues, they develop habits of doing the same. When we invite students to notice our mistakes and then react to those mistakes in positive ways, we create an environment where mistakes are seen as opportunities to learn. In essence, we need to maintain the Goldilocks principle of challenge: not too hard, not too easy, and not too boring. Many students will take on challenges if the task is not boring to them (which is why they so often enjoy their video games and sport).

Teach Positive Self-Talk

As the saying goes, it's really about mind over matter. We all give up when we start to tell ourselves that we can't do something anymore. In reality, we probably can continue, but when self-talk becomes negative, we don't carry on; we stop. We succumb to the inner dialogue of defeat. Instead, we must engage in positive self-talk. Consequently, we need to teach students to practice positive self-talk. Students have to learn how

Effective teachers use a gradual release of responsibility framework to support students' learning.

CHAPTER 3

to use this type of inner speech to keep themselves motivated. When students can tell themselves "I will read this one more time to figure out what the author is saying" or "I have done harder problems before; this one can't get me" or "I will stay with this at least five more minutes," this approach can go a long way in building grit and stamina.

Remind Them About Their Brains

Most students have not heard of plasticity, the understanding that the brain changes based on how it is used. Reminding students that they get better and better at the tasks by trying them and learning from their mistakes can be a powerful motivator for continued focus. And reminding them of their brilliant multilingual brains that are juggling multiple languages and communication systems builds on the strengths students bring to the classroom. They need to know about the bilingual advantage (e.g., van den Noort et al., 2019). Literally, the brain changes based on how it is used. Building stamina requires changes in the brain that simply don't occur from a single task. It's a much slower process, with slight increases in stamina each time the task requires a bit more.

Conclusion

This chapter has focused on challenge. Too often, multilingual learners experience lessons that do not challenge their thinking. Instead, lessons are overly differentiated and expectations are lowered. Although multilingual learners are doing double work—that is, learning language and content at the same time—the expectations for their learning should not be compromised. Instead, as we will see in the next chapter, teachers can focus on both language and content in the same lesson, developing students' linguistic skills as they learn content. We recognize that it takes time to learn in another language and that challenges are often increased when the learning occurs in another language. However, following an approach that sets high expectations for student learning and then aligns the instruction with those expectations is the best way forward.

When we invite students to notice our mistakes and then react to those mistakes in positive ways, we create an environment where mistakes are seen as opportunities to learn.

CHAPTER 3

Clarity of Learning

4

///

Big Idea

Multilingual learners have a lot to pay attention to, and they deserve to know what is important and valuable for their learning, in terms of content and language.

Questions Educators Ask

- How do I decide what students need to learn?

- What does it mean to teach with clarity?

- What role do standards play in multilingual students' learning expectations?

- How do I know if my students are successful?

Buckingham (2005), the strengths-focused business consultant, suggests that great leaders use optimism "to transform our fear of the unknown into confidence in the future" (p. 145). He also likes to say, "Clarity is the antidote to anxiety" (Buckingham, 2005, p. 146). Teachers are leaders of learning for their students, and we believe these two quotes are critical in the educational experiences of multilingual learners. As leaders, we must design learning experiences with optimism for our students' futures, and it is essential for us to ensure that we are clear in all aspects of the learning experiences. As Brown (2018), another leadership expert, reminds us, "Clear is kind. Unclear is unkind." Sage advice for teachers.

> We must design learning experiences with optimism for our students' futures.

Enter Teacher Clarity

Research on teacher clarity has existed for decades. It was described by Rosenshine and Furst (1971) as a critical factor in students' learning. When they identified eleven general categories of teacher behavior, they noted that teacher clarity topped the list in terms of impact on students' learning. The components of teacher clarity that they identified included

1. The clarity of the presentation is apparent to the students.

2. The points the teacher makes are clear and easy to understand.

3. The teacher explains concepts clearly and answers questions intelligently.

4. The lesson is organized.

Consider the following quotes in which various researchers explain *clarity*:

- "A cluster of teaching behaviors that result in learners gaining knowledge or understanding of a topic" (Cruickshank & Kennedy, 1986, p. 43).

- "Clarity, then, is the teacher's ability to present knowledge in a way that students can understand" (Simonds, 1997, p. 279).

- "Making content clear and accessible to students" (Saphier et al., 2008, p. 3).

- "A state in which a teacher who is in command of the subject matter to be transmitted is able to do that which is required to communicate with learners successfully" (Hines et al., 1985, p. 88).

We present these varied definitions because they each contribute to our understanding of this concept and highlight some essential aspects of learning experiences critical for multilingual learners. The first quote reminds us that students gain new knowledge from the lessons we design. The second indicates that the information must be presented in a way that is accessible to students. The third quote prompts us to note that it's the teacher's responsibility to make sure that the content is accessible. The last one reminds us that teachers must communicate effectively with students in a way that ensures learners develop a deeper understanding of the content.

Importantly, teacher clarity involves more than the expectations for learning, which we call *learning intentions* and *success criteria*. Others use the terms *learning goals, objectives, targets,* or *expectations.* We are not hung up on the semantics. The point is that students know what they are learning, and the lessons are organized so that they learn more. Building on the work of Rosenshine and Furst (1971), Fendick (1990) performed a meta-analysis of research studies and organized the evidence on teacher clarity into four categories:

- **Clarity of organization:** Tasks, assignments, and activities include links to the objectives and outcomes of learning (what we call *learning intentions* and *success criteria*).

- **Clarity of explanation:** Information is relevant, accurate, and comprehensible to students.

- **Clarity of examples and guided practice:** The lesson includes illustrative and illuminating information as students gradually move to independence, making progress with less support from the teacher.

- **Clarity of assessment of student learning:** The teacher regularly seeks out and acts upon the feedback they receive from students, especially through students' verbal and written responses.

When we know what success looks like, lessons are more likely to be organized.

By implication, teachers and students also need clarity about what success looks like. What does it mean to have learned something, and how do we know? When we know what success looks like, lessons are more likely to be organized; explanations, examples, and practice are more likely to be aligned; and assessments are more likely to focus on what was taught and not things we assume students know.

Teacher clarity has a respectable effect size of 0.84. In other words, it's a potential accelerator of students' learning. Consider the following questions: *Do your students know what they are supposed to be learning? Or do they see the class as a list of things to do?* There is a big difference between these two. Importantly, teachers do not get to decide if they are teaching with clarity; the students do.

When students know what they are expected to learn, they are more likely to learn it. At some point in every lesson, students should know what they are supposed to learn. Before we go much further into this topic, it's important to note the first part of the last sentence. We did not say, "At the outset of the lessons, students should know what they are learning." Rather, *at some point* they should.

There are a few valid reasons for withholding the purpose, or learning intention, until later in the lesson. Let's look at an example of a sixth-grade class that is learning about tectonic plates. Mr. Ramirez, their teacher, shows them several videos, and he shares a few short informational texts. During class, Mr. Ramirez guides students through a discussion about what they know about earthquakes and volcanoes, and each student creates a graphic organizer. Then he lets them know the lesson's purpose: to summarize major California landforms and movement along plates. The topics include plate boundaries, density, convection, subduction, trench, compression, ridge, and so on. The learning intentions do not focus on tectonic plates, but rather on summarizing information.

In this example, Mr. Ramirez wants to build students' background knowledge before focusing on the expected learning. As we will explore later in this chapter, language learning is always part of the expectations we have for multilingual learners.

Start With What Success Looks Like

Lessons don't just "happen"; they are the product of careful planning as teachers consider the long-term content goals and transfer skills their students need. Academic success is measured in part based on the content standards. Standards represent the official curriculum that schools must provide for students. They guide the instructional decision making for teachers who work to implement the curriculum. Often, teachers use instructional materials that are aligned with the standards. (Well, they are supposed to be aligned, anyway!) These materials include textbooks, supplemental materials, and online resources.

In some cases, the authors of the instructional materials have analyzed the standards and created learning expectations. Sometimes the textbooks have good learning intentions and success criteria, and other times they're not so good. And sometimes teachers want to reorganize the materials to create a pathway for learning for their students. To our thinking, teachers must know the standards for their grade or subject area if they are going to make informed decisions about learning expectations and assessments. They also need to know the language development and acquisition standards.

Some states have identified benchmarks or expectations that can be used to guide instruction for multilingual learners. These English language development standards are aligned to the English language arts standards, but they note appropriate language learning expectations for students' language proficiency levels. If your state does not have language development standards, the standards from WIDA are useful in planning (wida.wisc.edu). In addition to describing standards for the use of language in social and academic settings, they incorporate the use of

Teachers must know the standards if they are going to make informed decisions about learning expectations and assessments.

learning strategies to extend communicative competence, academic content knowledge, and sociolinguistic and sociocultural competence.

There are several ways to analyze standards. A simple way is to look at the standards' nouns (or noun phrases) and verbs (or verb phrases). This provides clarity about the concepts (nouns) and skills (verbs) that students must master. This analysis can also help teachers understand the type of thinking required or the depth of knowledge needed to be successful. For example, some standards focus on one idea, while others focus on several ideas. And still others focus on how ideas relate to one another or how ideas can be extended.

For example, in grade 3 of the California English Language Development Standards (California Department of Education, 2012), which are organized into three proficiency levels, students are expected to meet these expectations:

- **Emerging:** Plan and deliver very brief oral presentations (e.g., retelling a story, describing an animal, and the like)

- **Expanding:** Plan and deliver brief oral presentations on a variety of topics and content areas (e.g., retelling a story, explaining a science process, and the like)

- **Bridging:** Plan and deliver longer oral presentations on a variety of topics and content areas (e.g., retelling a story, explaining a science process or historical event, and the like)

Of course, a teacher might have students at every proficiency level in the class; in that case, the teacher will need to design opportunities for students to demonstrate these skills. Notice that the proficiency levels have some factors in common, as noted in the following table. The details that differ focus on the length of the presentation and the variety of topics and content.

CONCEPTS (NOUNS)	SKILLS (VERBS)
(Very) brief oral presentations (or longer)	Plan and deliver
	Retelling a story
	Describing
	Explaining

CHAPTER 4

This language development standard can be applied to any number of content standards in grade 3, such as

- Describe the economy and systems of government, particularly those with tribal constitutions, and their relationship to federal and state governments. (History/social studies)

- Conduct short research projects that build knowledge about a topic. (English language arts)

- Construct an argument that some animals form groups that help members survive. (Science)

- Demonstrate and explain how the selection of music to perform is influenced by personal interest, knowledge, purpose, and context. (Arts)

- Explain the purpose of warming up before physical activity and cooling down after physical activity. (Physical education)

Each of these would be analyzed the same, with verbs and nouns to identify the skills and concepts that students need to learn. Of course, this process applies to all grade levels and content areas. The key is to recognize that there are skills that students need to develop and concepts they need to learn—and the path to that learning is language: reading, writing, speaking, and listening.

Design Daily Learning Intentions and Success Criteria

As part of each lesson, students should know what they are expected to learn. We have organized this into three questions that contribute to teacher clarity (Fisher et al., 2016):

- What am I learning today?

- Why am I learning it?

- How will I know that I learned it?

The first question focuses on the learning intention, the second on the relevance, and the third on the ways in which students know what it means to learn something. We'll start with the learning intentions. Learning is hard work, and it's even harder for most multilingual students because they are doing "double the work" of everyone else (Short & Fitzsimmons, 2007). However, it's possible to mitigate this phenomenon by

1. Establishing the learning intention during the lesson

2. Returning to it throughout to redirect students

3. Using it to facilitate transitions

4. Using it as closure at the close of the lesson

As Hill and Flynn (2006) note, the learning environment "becomes a friendlier place for ELLs when they have a clearly stated target for learning" (p. 22). Identified and reclassified multilingual learners benefit from the clarity that comes when their teachers describe the learning expectations.

The learning intentions are derived from the standards, but they do not represent the entire standard. Rather, the intention is the content that will be learned within a single lesson. For instance, the broad standard might be to understand that variations in the characteristics of organisms can provide them advantages in survival, finding mates, and reproducing. In contrast, a single day's learning intention might be to identify how some insects use camouflage to hide from predators. The standard itself is important, of course, but it is also imperative that students know what they will be learning about *today*.

Students also need to know what successful learning looks like. In fact, when students understand how they will know that they learned something, they are more likely to do the following:

- Plan and predict what will happen in the class

- Set goals for themselves

- Accurately judge their own progress

- Know what is expected from them

- Feel safe

Each of these is a worthwhile goal for students, but be sure to note the last one. When students, especially multilingual learners, are anxious about their learning and their affective filter is raised, they learn less. The affective filter is often thought of as an imaginary wall that rises and blocks learning. As Krashen (1986) noted, our affective filters are influenced by our motivation, self-confidence, and anxiety. Clarity, especially in terms of what successful learning looks like, can help lower that imaginary wall and increase students' comfort with the learning tasks.

CHAPTER 4

The learning intentions name the destination; the success criteria provide a means for teachers and students to utilize feedback specifically oriented to the learning intentions. The success criteria make it apparent how a task, assignment, or project will be judged. One common method of articulating success criteria uses "I Can" statements, such as these:

- I can name two words that rhyme.

- I can describe what happens when two forces act on an object in opposing directions.

- I can identify primary and secondary sources.

These statements are of lesser value when they are isolated. For instance, identifying sources is only one step in terms of learning about historical events. Students also need to be able to use these sources to analyze historical decisions, determine bias in the documents, analyze the credibility of the sources, and so on.

For this reason, many teachers use rubrics to articulate a constellation of quality indicators. Another type of success criteria is a list of deliverables for a project, again with quality indicators for each item. This type of success criteria states the necessary elements of the project, but it also serves as more than a simple to-do checklist because it challenges students to assess for quality, not just compliance.

The success criteria come from a variety of sources, and students need to know what successful learning of the content means. For example, consider the following learning intention from a middle school English class:

I am learning about the way writers use figurative language.

A range of success criteria may be used, depending on the amount of previous learning students have done and how much time is devoted to the lesson. Here are several examples of success criteria that align with this learning intention:

- I can find examples of figurative language in a text.

- I can explain to my partner what the figurative language means.

- I can identify the reason the author might have used the figurative language.

- I can infer a reader's emotional response to the figurative language.

- I can use figurative language in my writing.

CHAPTER 4

Notice that the first examples are less rigorous than the later examples, but they are foundational and critical to the growing success of students. Also notice that they are grounded in language. Students are using language functions in this case to demonstrate their success.

One way teachers can integrate content and language expectations for multilingual learners is to ensure that the success criteria require that students produce language. In a study of more than three hundred teachers of multilingual learners (Fisher & Frey, 2010), we identified the following three types of language expectations:

Ensure that the success criteria require that students produce language.

- **Vocabulary:** Probably the most common type of language expectation is based on the vocabulary that students need to know. When teachers analyze their lessons, they may notice that specialized words—words with multiple meanings—need attention. For example, a lesson on the human body includes words such as *tissue, vessel,* and *feet* that have multiple meanings. Alternatively, when teachers analyze their lessons, they will notice that technical words—words specific to the discipline—need attention. For example, the lesson on the human body also includes *trachea, alveoli,* and *esophagus.* The success criteria could focus on either specialized or technical words, though probably on different days.

- **Structure:** The English language has a structure that students must come to understand. Accordingly, teachers can develop success criteria to ensure students learn grammar and syntax. For example, teachers might focus on subject and verb agreement in students' talk or ask them to use signal words, such as *first, next, then,* and *finally,* in their writing. By attending to the structure of the language, multilingual learners begin to generalize their understanding of the language conventions.

- **Function:** Language is used for a purpose, whether to inform, entertain, persuade, or accomplish a host of other reasons. Helping students match their speaking and writing with a specific function requires sophisticated thinking and planning. When students understand the expected language function, they are tasked with remaining true to that function and developing their ideas.

Figure 4.1 contains examples of language expectations from various content areas. Our purpose here is to remind educators that achievement rises when students know what to pay attention to. This is consistent with the findings of Echevarria et al. (2006) who found that analysis of the language demand of the task, paired with stated

CHAPTER 4

purposes about written and verbal language production, resulted in higher levels of achievement for multilingual learners.

FIGURE 4.1	Language Purpose Statements From Four Content Areas		
CONTENT AREA	**VOCABULARY**	**STRUCTURE**	**FUNCTION**
Mathematics	Use *less than, equal to,* or *greater than* to compare groups or numbers.	Use the language frame "The answer ____ is/is not reasonable because ____."	Describe the relationship between numbers in expanded form and standard form.
Social Studies	Name the routes and explorers on a map.	Sequence the steps of food production using the signal words *first, then, next,* and *finally.*	Justify in a paragraph the ways fire was used for hunting, cooking, and warmth by citing three examples.
Language Arts	Use *who, what,* and *why* to ask a question of your partner.	Identify the verb tenses used in the reading to explain what happened long ago and what will happen in the future.	Explain what organizational pattern was used by the writer and critique its adequacy.
Science	Label a diagram of the digestive system (*teeth, mouth, esophagus, stomach, small intestine, large intestine, colon*).	Using the sentence frame "On the one hand . . . On the other hand," students will demonstrate their knowledge of the earth's layers.	I can tell my team members three ways that an environment can change.

Source: Fisher and Frey (2010).

Notice that these success criteria serve as a bridge between what will be learned (the content or learning intention) and what the students will be doing (the task). In the case of the third-grade science lesson, the vocabulary demand might include *disguise, blending*, and, of course, *camouflage.*

Another related lesson might have a different language purpose, this time using the language's structure, syntax, and grammar. For instance, if a major task involves writing, the language demand might be to "summarize the article about stick insects using a paragraph frame to describe how it uses camouflage." Then the paragraph frame might look like this:

> The (organism) is a/an (describe the organism) that is able to hide from predators. The (organism) is able to do this by (explain how this is done). Predators like (organism) are fooled because (explain what confuses the predator). This keeps the (organism) safe.

Using sentence and paragraph frames provides a scaffold for multilingual learners to correctly structure written and spoken language as they engage with content. As students internalize these language frames, teachers should introduce new and more sophisticated ones. With that in mind, these frames should not remain in place for the entire school year but evolve in complexity as language learners grow. The goal is not to limit students to a strict and rigid adherence to the frames, but rather to assist them in building a repertoire of ways they can convey experiences, information, and opinions.

The third facet of language expectations is the function. Functions of school language include expressing an opinion, describing a phenomenon, summarizing a text passage, persuading an audience, and providing justification or reasoning. Vocabulary and structure purposes, as described previously, almost always name a function within it, as in *summarizing* an article. But there are instances when the function, rather than the vocabulary or structural demands, are foregrounded, as when the third-grade science teacher informs her students that they will be comparing the ways two different species disguise themselves.

There is another facet useful in learning tasks: ensuring that students understand the social demands of the lesson. Success criteria can include the social skills that students are learning. Younger children, those who are new to a school or classroom, and students with limited experience benefit tremendously from social purposes that target the nonverbal

Using sentence and paragraph frames provides a scaffold for multilingual learners to correctly structure written and spoken language.

communication skills needed. These can include—but are not limited to—tracking the speaker, making eye contact, and listening while others speak.

All students, regardless of age and experience, need to be apprenticed into the speaking and listening skills associated with their grade levels. As well, it is important to understand the cultural and linguistic experiences and assets of children, particularly in light of what they are learning. For example, middle school students need to learn how to work with a group to set project goals and deadlines. High school students need to learn how to incorporate the ideas of others in discussions, and they need to learn how to challenge ideas and conclusions without being disagreeable.

Returning to the third-grade science lesson one last time, a social purpose in the lesson might be for students to ask questions of the teacher and of their peers to check their own understanding of the topic of the lesson. As another example, here's an assignment focused on a controversial topic in high school science:

> Today we are learning to identify your reasons either in support of, or in opposition to, keeping animals in captivity. You will discuss the reasons with your group, listen carefully to the reasons of others, monitor your emotional reactions if you disagree, and provide useful verbal feedback to each other. In order to get the most from the feedback, you will take notes about the feedback you receive in preparation for writing your letter.

We can break this assignment down into parts:

Learning intention: Students must identify their reasons either in support of, or in opposition to, keeping animals in captivity.

Language success criteria: Students must discuss the reasons with their group, provide useful verbal feedback to each other, and take notes about the feedback they receive.

Social success criteria: Students must listen carefully to the reasons of others and monitor their emotional reactions if they disagree.

Figure 4.2 contains the learning intentions and success criteria used on one day in a junior high school. We are not suggesting that these are perfect, but this example serves as a reflection of the authentic learning that was expected of students across the day.

All students, regardless of age and experience, need to be apprenticed into the speaking and listening skills associated with their grade levels.

CHAPTER 4

FIGURE 4.2 Sample Learning Intentions (LI) and Success Criteria (SC)

	ENGLISH LANGUAGE ARTS	SCIENCE	MATH	SOCIAL STUDIES	ART AND MUSIC
Seventh Grade	**LI:** We are learning how a red herring affects a story's plot. **SC:** I can define *red herring*, using examples from my own reading. I can find at least one example in the text that I am reading. I can discuss with my group the reasons why the author might have used it. I can take turns and ask related questions of my group.	**LI:** We are learning about cell organelles and how they support the function of the cell. **SC:** I can compare the functions of a cell wall and a cell membrane. I can explain to my partner why some cells have a cell wall while others do not. I can demonstrate that I value the ideas and opinions of others.	**LI:** We are learning about simple interest. **SC:** I can explain the relationship between principal and interest when requesting a loan. I can calculate simple interest. I can ask and answer questions.	**LI:** We are learning about the establishment of Spanish colonies in the Americas. **SC:** I can analyze the impact of exploration and colonization on Indigenous Peoples. I can describe the lasting impact of colonization on Indigenous Peoples. I can ensure that everyone has an opportunity to share.	**LI:** We are learning how musicians improve the quality of their creative work. **SC:** I can describe the rationale for making revisions to music based on specific criteria. I can hypothesize why specific artists revise their work and the impact of those revisions. I can monitor my impact on others when I share.
Eighth Grade	**LI:** We are learning about how to use alliteration as a literary device. **SC:** I can include an example of alliteration in my writing. I can explain how the use of alliteration enhanced my own writing. I can politely disagree with others and maintain our group cohesion.	**LI:** We are learning how elements are arranged on the Periodic Table. **SC:** I can determine the number of energy levels in an atom. I can explain how energy levels influence the behavior of atoms. I can explain the relationship between energy levels and the placement of the elements on the Periodic Table to my peers. I can practice using an inside voice.	**LI:** We are learning about rigid transformations. **SC:** I can describe what is meant by a rigid transformation. I can use the Pythagorean theorem to find the perimeter of a triangle. I can ask for help when I am not sure about the information.	**LI:** We are learning about events that led to the Revolutionary War. **SC:** I can describe the significance of the Stamp Act, citing evidence from historical sources. I can explain how many Colonists reacted to the Stamp Act. I can describe the relationship of the Stamp Act to other key events leading to the Revolutionary War. I can work to reach consensus and identify places where we don't agree.	**LI:** We are learning how artists may follow or break from established traditions. **SC:** I can provide an example of an artist who took a risk to pursue an idea. I can explain how this particular artist followed or broke established traditions. I can describe the impact of this decision on their artwork. I can actively listen, even when I do not agree with the person speaking.

Find the Relevance

Thus far, we have focused on two of the clarity questions we identified previously: *What are we learning today?* And *How do we know that we learned it?* The middle question—*Why are we learning this?*—has plagued educators for decades. We all know that boredom is a problem; as we have noted, being bored in school has significant negative impacts on learning, with an effect size of −0.46. To counter that, teachers need to find ways to make learning relevant for students.

Students with high levels of self-regulation tend to find relevance in a lot of the learning they're introduced to, but students who have low levels of self-regulation need help finding relevance. Further, what is relevant to one person may not be relevant to another. Priniski et al. (2018) conceptualize relevance across a continuum from least to most relevant. We have defined these levels of relevance as follows:

- **Personal association** occurs through a connection to an object or a memory, such as when students enjoy an article about travel because they recall riding in an airplane when they were younger. Similarly, personal association occurs when students make a connection with something outside the classroom and thus want to learn more.

- **Personal usefulness** occurs when students believe that a task or text will help them reach a personal goal. For example, children may read articles about soccer because they want to improve their passing skills. Similarly, students might persevere through a challenging mathematics course because they believe that the knowledge will help them gain admission to a specific college, thus allowing them to study engineering.

- **Personal identification** is the most motivating type of relevancy; it stems from students' deep understanding that the task or text aligns with their identity. When students get to learn about themselves, their problem solving, and their ability to impact others, relevance is increased. For example, students who want to build shelters for stray cats are highly motivated to learn geometry. Students who see themselves as poets seek feedback and lessons about voice, ideas, and organization.

Let's look at another example to show how personal relevance plays out in the classroom. Amie Carter, who teaches fourth grade in a dual language program in which about half of her students speak English and home and half speak Spanish at home, knows that her students love stories. When she introduces a new story to her students, she asks them questions that help them identify goals. For example, she asked students why readers tend to focus on the characters. The range of responses on a given day included the following:

- "Because we want to write stories, too."

- "Because when we see how characters feel, we understand why they do things."

- "Because characters help us think about our behavior."

- "Because characters have emotions, and so do we."

The students sat with rapt attention on the day their teacher started reading *When You Trap a Tiger* (Keller, 2020). The first line reads, "I can turn invisible." (If you know fourth graders, that's a pretty good hook.) Later, the class discussed one of the ideas from the book: "When you believe, that is you being brave. Sometimes, believing is the bravest thing of all" (p. 51). The lesson was relevant because students understood that they could reach their goals by participating in this lesson.

Similarly, the students in Jerrod Barlow's middle school science class find relevance in their lessons when their teachers talk with them about why they are learning certain things. He tries to make connections with students' personal identification. For example, in their unit on human body systems, Mr. Barlow regularly makes connections to sports and fitness goals, healthy living, and future careers, all things that his students have told him are important to them. For example, he says, "Our next system focuses on the brain, and we all know how important that is. But did you know that you can change your brain? Literally. You can change what is inside your head. It's about the connections inside our brains. Really, you can change it. Tonight. Want to know how?" They all put their thumbs up, ready to learn.

> We can't forget that students need to know what they are learning and how they will know if they are successful.

Conclusion

As we noted in the opening of this chapter, clarity is kind. We can't forget that students need to know what they are learning and how they will know if they are successful. By sharing this information with them, we reduce anxiety about learning and provide the necessary support for students to succeed. Of course, teacher clarity involves more than just learning intentions and success criteria, as we will explore in the next chapter. But clarity starts with knowing and sharing what your students need to learn, in terms of content and language, and inviting them into various learning opportunities to make sure that learning happens.

CHAPTER 4

Cohesion in Learning

5

It's a beautiful thing to be in the presence of a masterful teacher of multilingual students who is concise, who is precise, and who doesn't overlook the nuances that belie students' learning and confusion. Such teachers exhibit a high level of clarity as they communicate the learning intentions and success criteria to students; use questions, prompts, and cues to guide their students' learning; create opportunities for students to collaborate with peers in meaningful ways; and utilize independent learning to extend and deepen students' knowledge and skills. Each of these actions is an intentional step that builds student competence and confidence in their learning.

There was a time when "learning" was seen as a black box; educators and researchers were not sure how it operated. As a profession, we recognized that there were inputs that likely assisted with learning and outputs that allowed us to check to see if learning occurred, but the process of learning itself was unclear.

Fast-forward several decades, and we know a lot about learning for multilingual learners. Language is crucial for cognition, and multilingual learners are doubly challenged in terms of how they allocate cognitive resources when learning. As one example, students reading in a second language may find retrieving information from an earlier part of the text more difficult, and therefore they may have lower comprehension (Morishima, 2013). In this case, it isn't a matter of not being able to understand the story, but rather they have reached cognitive overload because they must dedicate increased attention to what they are reading in the moment. This has direct implications for instruction. Breaking the reading into smaller chunks, with opportunities to discuss incrementally, can aid in text comprehension. The good news is that there's a process for that: reciprocal teaching (Palincsar & Brown, 1984).

Quality Core Instruction for Multilingual Learners

We recognize that there are specific instructional moves that successful teachers make to increase the likelihood that multilingual students learn. A dominant theory in this area is the gradual release of responsibility, which suggests that educators intentionally and purposefully design learning experiences and then move along this trajectory: (1) assuming all the responsibility for learning; (2) sharing responsibility for learning; (3) ensuring that students have increasing levels of cognitive responsible for their learning (Fisher & Frey, 2021; Pearson & Gallagher, 1983). This trajectory occurs on multiple levels, from the lesson to the week to the unit to the year. Broadly speaking, these moves include the following:

- **Teachers model and demonstrate through focused instruction.** This approach allows students an apprenticeship opportunity to try on the cognitive and metacognitive moves of others. This does not have to come first in the lesson, but students do need examples of the thinking required for the task. Teachers can ask themselves what students need to see or experience from their teachers and which types of modeling, worked examples, or think-alouds will help. This is where students receive input and information, but with examples of the thinking provided. It's not simply a lecture but rather a demonstration of the cognitive or metacognitive skills students need to develop.

- **Teachers guide students' thinking and learning** to address errors and misconceptions through prompts, cues, and questions without telling students the answers. This approach is commonly done in smaller groups, and it allows teachers to provide needed direct instruction or guided learning experiences. Typically, this process begins with a question, either from the teacher or the students. Teachers can prompt and cue students, providing just enough support for students to experience cognitive demand.

- **Teachers provide collaborative learning opportunities** that allow students to interact with peers, using academic language, to consolidate their understanding.

- **Teachers assign independent learning tasks** that allow students to practice and apply what they have learned.

Of course, these moves require opportunities for elaborate encoding and retrieval practice, and educators need to collect evidence of students' learning. In these ways, educators monitor their impact on students' learning and adjust their actions to increase that impact. When these forces are at play, student learning accelerates. Throughout this chapter, we'll explore each of these steps in more detail, spotlighting specific language strategies that can be useful in accelerating the achievement of multilingual learners.

Focused Instruction for Multilingual Learners

A chief role of focused instruction is to provide input that students can then use collaboratively or individually. This is accomplished through several instructional moves, including

- Ensuring students know what they are learning through teacher clarity

- Providing direct instruction, videos, or lectures

- Modeling and demonstrating to students how a concept is utilized

One area of need for multilingual learners involves learning to navigate the structure of the language through the lens of grammar. Grammatical differences are evidenced in speaking and in writing, and while teachers may detect those differences, they may be unsure how to address them in ways that encourage, rather than discourage, communication. Figure 5.1 provides a brief overview of common differences that are manifested in English.

FIGURE 5.1 Common Grammatical Differences of Multilingual Learners		
RULE OF STANDARD ENGLISH GRAMMAR	**EXAMPLE**	**NONEXAMPLE**
Sentence Structure: All simple sentences have one subject and one main verb. A main verb is not a part of an infinitive that begins with *to*.	My English <u>teacher</u> in high school was <u>the key person</u> who taught me.	My English <u>teacher</u> in high school <u>key person</u> who taught me.
Subject–Verb Agreement: Subjects agree with verbs in number. Infinite pronouns such as *everyone* are generally followed by singular verbs.	Everyone <u>understands</u> me.	Everyone <u>understand</u> me.
Verb Tense: Use the present tense to refer to events that happen now and to indicate general truth. Use the past tense to refer to events that took place in the past. Generally, use present perfect with words such as *already*, *yet*, and *since*.	My teacher <u>explained</u> how important books are for students.	My teacher <u>explain</u> to me that how important books was for the student.
Verb Phrases: Certain verbs are followed by *to* plus the base form of the verb; others are followed by a verb that ends in *-ing*.	My teacher persuaded me <u>to read</u> many books.	My teacher persuaded me <u>read</u> many book.
Plurals: A plural count noun (*table*, *book*, *pencil*) ends in a *-s*.	My teacher persuaded me to read many <u>books</u>.	My teacher persuaded me to read many <u>book</u>.
Auxiliaries: Negative sentences are formed by using *do* + *not* + the base form of the word.	Please <u>do not make</u> me lose face.	Please <u>do not makes</u> me lose face.
Articles: Definitive articles generally precede specific nouns that are easily identifiable because they are modified by adjectives.	I don't speak <u>the Vietnamese</u> language.	I don't speak <u>the Vietnam</u> language.
Word Forms: The standard parts of speech should be used (e.g., nouns as nouns, verbs as verbs).	I have <u>confidence</u> in English.	I have <u>confident</u> in English.
Fixed Expressions and Idioms: Idioms and fixed expressions cannot be changed in any way.	Please do not make me <u>lose face</u>.	Please do not make me <u>lose the face</u>.
Word Choice: Formal words should be used in formal settings. Informal words should be used in informal settings.	Dear <u>Professor Scarcella</u>:	Dear <u>Robbin</u>:

Source: Adapted from Scarcella (2000).

Every language has grammar, which are the rules that govern it, and there has been a revitalization of English grammar instruction as teachers look for ways to support multilingual learners. However, because of differences in the grammar of languages, multilingual students can get confused. As examples of these differences, many Asian languages do not use articles such as *a, an,* and *the*; Spanish nouns are gendered; and Somali has no perfect tenses. Even English grammar rules have many exceptions because the roots come from so many different languages.

At a social level, English grammar instruction is also riddled with concerns about the privileging of a standard for English versus the variations students may use at home, in their communities, and in settings outside the classroom. Specifically, when one version of English (referred to as standard English, or SE) is set up as the "correct" form, it perpetuates a wrongheaded message that other forms (vernacular English, or VE, as well as home languages) are "wrong" or "incorrect." The perspective that there is only one version of correct English results in a prescriptive form of grammar instruction that limits language use to standard English only. Consequently, it is not uncommon for multilingual learners to wrongly believe that their L1 is somehow less worthy or valued.

One successful approach that addresses some of these concerns is contrastive grammar analysis, which teaches multilingual learners to notice the grammar of their L1 or home language and then to compare this grammar to that of standard English. The emphasis of this approach is on descriptive, rather than prescriptive grammar. Contrastive grammar analysis moves students away from correctness and toward codeswitching, and it. A contrastive grammar analysis approach situates the merit of the language used in home and community. Figure 5.2 provides a comparison of a prescriptive grammar approach to a comparative analysis one.

Modeling and Demonstrating in a Contrastive Grammar Lesson

It's early in the school year, and second-grade teacher Valerie Petersen wants to situate her grammar instruction so that she can draw on a contrastive grammar analysis approach. Many of her students are multilingual learners, representing three different home languages. She sets the stage by enlisting three parents from the school's English Language Advisory Committee (ELAC)—Ms. Garcia, Mr. Nguyen, and Ms. Kassa—to help her demonstrate the approach for her students. Working with these adults, she plans the conversation in advance.

On the day of the demonstration, Ms. Petersen begins by telling her class that going to the food market is something each of the four adults

FIGURE 5.2	New Ways of Talking About Language: From "Error" to "Pattern"
INSTEAD OF THIS . . .	**TRY THIS . . .**
Thinking in terms of • Proper or improper • Good or bad	Seeing language as • Appropriate or inappropriate • Effective or ineffective in a specific setting
Talking about • Right or wrong • Correct or incorrect	Talking about • Patterns • How language varies by setting
Thinking that students • Make mistakes or errors • Have problems with plurals, possessives, tenses, etc. • Leave off -s, -es, -ed	Seeing your students as • Following the grammar patterns of their home language
Saying students • "Should have" or "are supposed to," "need to," "should correct"	Inviting students to • Codeswitch (choose the language pattern to fit the setting)
Making red notes in the margin • Correcting students' grammar	Leading students to • Compare and contrast languages • Build on existing knowledge to add new knowledge—standard English • Codeswitch to fit the setting

Source: Wheeler and Swords (2006, p. xvii). Copyright © 2006 by the National Council of Teachers of English. Adapted with permission.

does weekly. She says that sometimes she can't find an item and needs to ask an employee where the item is located. After demonstrating how she does so in English ("Where are some carrots, please?"), she invites each parent to model how they do so in Spanish, Vietnamese, and Oromo.

After each parent models posing the question in their home language, she asks them how they would do so if the employee spoke English only. Again, each parent poses a similar question, this time in English. Ms. Petersen notes that everyone asks the question in a slightly different way but that none of them is wrong. She tells the class, "Something I noticed is that the words in the sentences were a little bit different. Let's write down how each of us asked the question."

As the teacher writes on the chart paper, Ms. Garcia says that she asked where the *las zanahorias* (carrots) were. She adds that when she asked in English, she had to think about how to ask for more than one carrot, but she wasn't certain if she needed a word for *las*.

Mr. Nguyen asked for *cà rốt,* but he notes that because his home language doesn't use plurals, he had some difficulty with asking for more than one.

Ms. Kassa asked for *kaarotaa.* She explains that because there is no word for *some* in Oromo, when she asked the same question in English, she skipped that word altogether.

The teacher then provides some direct instruction for students so that they will further understand the process of contrastive grammar analysis. She says, "All of the languages we use have rules so that our questions make sense. But when we switch between languages, not all of the rules are the same. All of them are correct in one language, but because the rules are different in other languages, the way they are said may be different, too."

She briefly checks to make sure the children are following the discussion. Then she continues by saying, "When we talk to each other and write our ideas in English, there are rules to learn so we can make ideas clear. But we can also be 'pattern detectives.' As we learn about the rules in English, we're also going to look at how these patterns work in Spanish, Vietnamese, and Oromo. And when we are helping each other with our speaking and writing, we don't say, 'That is wrong.' Instead, we can say, 'Here's what that sounds like in English.' Let's add that idea to our list of how we help each other."

Guided Instruction for Multilingual Learners

The primary purpose of guided instruction is to operate in the learner's zone of proximal (and potential, we would add) development, or ZPD. ZPD is a theory that was first articulated by Russian developmental psychologist Lev Vygotsky (1978) in the 1920s but did not become well known until his work was translated decades later. Vygotsky's work focused on the relationship between language and thought. He championed the notion that development is a product of learning and that engaging in problem solving with a more capable peer or adult results in a higher function. Wood et al. (1976) further expanded on how this

The primary purpose of guided instruction is to operate in the learner's zone of proximal (and potential) development.

CHAPTER 5

occurs, naming these instructional practices as *scaffolding*. These scaffolds occur through a series of robust questions, prompts, and cues (Fisher & Frey, 2021). Scaffolding is a critical tool that teachers have to support multilingual learners (Fenner & Snyder, 2017).

Guided instruction affords multilingual students with opportunities to consolidate their developing linguistic skills. Because of the attention required on the part of the teacher, extended guided instruction occurs in small groups and with individual students. The teacher is continuously formulating hypotheses, such as *What does the student know and not know to lead them to that particular response? What might they be using but confusing?*

Language structure includes grammar, as discussed earlier, and it also includes syntax: the lining up of words such that they make sense. One example of a comprehensible sentence in English is *People write to communicate their ideas.* In Spanish, the sentence is *La gente escribe para comunicar sus ideas.* Now scramble the sentence in both languages: *Communicate ideas to write people their. Comunicar ideas para escribar la gente sus.* In each case, while the words are the same, the order renders them meaningless. Knowledge of syntax by multilingual learners correlates with reading comprehension (Gámez & Lesaux, 2012).

"Juicy sentences" is a close reading approach for multilingual learners developed by Fillmore and Fillmore (n.d.) to parse and slice complex sentences. This approach focuses on the metalanguage that may otherwise elude students, and it includes discussion about the intended audience and the function of the sentences, as well as how words, phrases, and clauses signal the meaning. The purpose is to assist multilingual students in unlocking the meaning of individual sentences—and therefore the meaning of the longer text itself.

Student Achievement Partners (n.d.), a nonprofit dedicated to educational supports in literacy and mathematics for students and their teachers, offers guidance on selecting a passage that is a good fit for the juicy sentence approach. It is not necessary for each of these conditions to be met in a single passage, but the material should meet these standards:

- It should come from grade-appropriate complex text.

- It should come from a text that is conceptually connected to content being discussed in class already. STEM, history, social studies, and ELA texts all make great candidates! This allows students to build on and reinforce the knowledge and vocabulary they've acquired from other texts.

Scaffolding is a critical tool that teachers have to support multilingual learners.

- It should have high informational density. That is, multiple pieces of information are contained in the sentence and/or can be construed from its subtext.

- It should be "chunkable" so teachers can break it apart into smaller sections for focused discussion. There isn't a rule about the exact right number of chunks or the right number of words or phrases that constitute a chunk, but teachers should think strategically about the ideas each chunk is conveying. Don't leave students hanging by splitting apart an idea into two chunks!

- It should feature language related to complex thought, where readers are asked to interpret motivation, rationale, time, place, contingencies related to actions, and so forth.

- It should feature grade-level academic language.

- It should contain complex noun phrases (nouns that are modified or expanded by other phrases).

- It should contain adverbial clauses.

- It should use passive voice.

- It should include linking phrases.

- It should introduce a metaphor or simile.

Fillmore and Fillmore note that juicy sentences should be selected from texts students are reading, in order to support them more completely in understanding the reading itself. In other words, these exercises are not isolated but are used to provide guidance on how language structures are used to make meaning in the sentences of the text. Let's look at an example of what this approach can look like in the classroom.

Ninth-grade ethnic studies teacher Martin Carter's main text is *A Young People's History of the United States* (Zinn, 2016). His current unit is on Christopher Columbus and other so-called explorers who wreaked havoc on the North American continent. Mr. Carter meets with a small group of multilingual learners to closely examine several sentences from the text that form an important concept: The Spaniards' invasion of what is now known as Haiti, driven by a search for gold, led to the murders of countless Arawak, the indigenous people of the island.

Mr. Carter leads the group in reading and discussing these sentences:

> When it was clear that there was no gold left, the Indians were enslaved on the Spaniards' huge estates. They were

Juicy sentences should be selected from texts students are reading in order to support them more completely in understanding the reading itself.

CHAPTER 5

overworked and mistreated, and they died by the thousands. By 1550, only five hundred Indians remained. A century later, no Arawaks were left on the island. (p. 10)

Mr. Carter helps the students parse the sentences by asking a series of robust questions, using a protocol developed by the Council of Great City Schools (n.d.):

- Whom or what is this all about? (subject/topic)

- What does it say about the who or what? (verb/predicate)

- What does this part say? What questions does it answer?

To follow up, he asks them to identify the part or parts that answer these questions:

- Where does this take place?

- When does this take place?

- Why did this happen?

- How did this happen?

Mr. Carter believes this approach is a great way to help his students. He notes, "These questions guide my discussion with them and keep me from telling them all the information. I don't have to spend a lot of time on this—maybe seven to ten minutes, max. But it gives me a way to circle up with those readers who need the text warmed up for them. And it keeps me on my toes because I get to see firsthand how they are processing the text and where confusion may lie. Funny thing is, it's rarely about content. It's usually a linguistic barrier that I can help them untangle."

Collaborative Learning for Multilingual Learners

To develop proficiency in a language, students must practice using the language. Collaborative learning is an important aspect of quality instruction for all students, as it shifts the cognitive responsibility to students to produce language using the academic concepts they are learning. While multilingual students are developing their language proficiency through oral language practice, they can develop their

Opportunities to talk give students much needed time to process the concepts being taught.

content knowledge. Opportunities to talk give students much-needed time to process the concepts being taught.

Swain (1995) suggests that when multilingual students are required to produce language, they process it at a deeper level than when they merely listen. As they clarify their meaning to make it understandable to others, they must stretch their language resources, thereby developing their proficiency. When talk incorporates opportunities for students to interact in ways that require them to use academic language, students not only practice the language they already control but also are stretched to extend their skills to higher levels in order to communicate.

These discussions require that students engage in exploratory talk (Mercer & Wegerif, 2004). Students question and clarify, revise their thinking based on input from others, and develop deeper understandings. However, don't confuse any old talk at all with productive talk. Here's their definition of exploratory talk:

> *Exploratory talk* occurs when partners engage critically but constructively with each other's ideas. Statements and suggestions are offered for joint consideration. These may be challenged and counter-challenged, but challenges are justified and alternative hypotheses are offered. Partners all actively participate, and opinions are sought and considered before decisions are jointly made. Exploratory talk knowledge is made more publicly accountable and reasoning is more visible in the talk. (Mercer & Wegerif, 2004, p. 72)

The authors contrast exploratory talk with two other types of discourse that may be of less value:

> *Disputational talk* . . . is characterized by disagreement and individualized decision making. There are few attempts to pool resources, offer constructive criticism, or make suggestions. Disputational talk also has some characteristic discourse features—short exchanges consisting of assertions and challenges or counter assertions. *Cumulative talk* [happens when] speakers build positively but uncritically on what the others have said. Partners use talk to construct common knowledge by accumulation. Cumulative discourse is characterized by repetitions, confirmations, and elaborations. (Mercer & Wegerif, 2004, p. 72)

When multilingual students are required to produce language, they process it at a deeper level than when they merely listen.

CHAPTER 5

Fostering Exploratory Talk
Through Collaborative Learning

Eighth-grade science teacher Kyle Russo uses reciprocal teaching (RT) so that students work through textbook readings together. RT is an approach that was developed by Palincsar and Brown (1984), and it mirrors the major reading comprehension processes used to make meaning from text. Students read a short segment of text (often one to three paragraphs in length) and take turns asking questions, clarifying, summarizing, predicting, and visualizing at the end of each segment.

RT has a robust effect size of 0.74, so it has good potential to accelerate learning. This strategy is particularly valuable for multilingual learners using expository text because they find support for comprehension through small-group interaction (Casey, 2018). Because longer texts are segmented into shorter passages and punctuated by discussion, multilingual learners in the group are better able to comprehend more complex sequences of cumulative information that build upon each other over the course of the reading.

Mr. Russo and other members of the eighth-grade team taught the reciprocal teaching protocol to their students during the first month of school. Each student has an assigned role for the reading:

- **Question:** Questioning helps to check for comprehension in addition to deepening understanding. The questioner poses questions drawn from the segment they have just read.

- **Clarify:** Students may need to clarify unfamiliar vocabulary, a new or difficult concept, or the structure of the text or the meaning. The clarifier moderates how the members assist each other by explaining, rereading, or using outside resources such as a glossary.

- **Summarize:** Students integrate the ideas and identify the main points and supporting information in the text. The summarizer may use a graphic organizer or take notes to help the members organize the information.

- **Predict:** Students use what they have read along with their prior knowledge about the topic and the type of text to predict what they might read next. Predicting helps to set a purpose for reading as students confirm or reject their hypotheses. The predictor asks what the group's predictions are for the next section, especially in speculating what the author will tell them next.

Mr. Russo groups the students heterogeneously so they can support each other, both for content and for language. He uses this approach with the students once a week with their major reading, and the notes the students generate with their RT group become a part of the writing they do for the class.

Teachers should ensure discussion routines fostering exploratory talk also require students to engage using higher-order thinking skills. Language frames are quite useful for ensuring students know how to engage in higher-order discussion, rather than disputational or cumulative talk. Mr. Russo uses provides students with frames aligned to the RT roles in order to encourage exploratory talk (see Figure 5.3).

Language frames are useful for ensuring students know how to engage in higher-order discussion.

FIGURE 5.3 Language Frames for Reciprocal Teaching

CLARIFY	SUMMARIZE
We clear up confusion and find meaning for unfamiliar words, sentences, ideas, or concepts.	*We restate the main ideas, events, or points.*
This is confusing to me . . .	A good summary includes
I need to reread, slow down, look at the graphs or illustrations, or break the word apart.	• Key people, items, or places
	• Key words and synonyms
When I began reading this, I thought . . .	• Key ideas and concepts
Then, when I read this part, I realized . . .	The main point is . . .
	If I put the ideas together, I now understand that . . .
It didn't make sense until I . . .	The most important thing I read was . . .

PREDICTION	QUESTION
We look and listen for clues that will tell us what may happen next and what we can expect to learn in the next section of the text.	*We test ourselves about what we just read by asking ourselves questions. We see if we really understand and can identify what is important.*
Good predictions are based on . . .	We ask ourselves different questions and reflect:
• What we already know	• Factual questions: Who, what, when, where?
• What we understand from the text	• Interpretive questions: How? Why?
• What the pictures, charts, or graphs tell us	• Reflective statements: I wonder . . . . I'm curious about . . .
I think . . .	
I predict . . .	
I bet . . .	
I wonder . . .	

CHAPTER 5

Independent Learning for Multilingual Learners

Learning shouldn't stop when independent work begins. This seems obvious, but in too many classrooms the independent tasks and the thinking required to complete them are limited to the regurgitation of knowledge. The work itself doesn't forward students' learning; it is simply assigned to determine how closely their factual knowledge pairs with what the teacher has taught. Instead, teachers need to aim for three quality indicators that deepen learning in the independent phase of instruction: the opportunity to think metacognitively, the chance to set goals, and the opportunity to develop self-regulatory skills. Let's look at three questions teachers can use to evaluate the tasks they assign and make sure they promote continued learning.

Does It Promote Metacognition?

The first question to pose about an independent task is whether it promotes metacognition. Self-awareness about learning evolves over a lifetime, and students can begin to form this beneficial habit through opportunities to examine their own thinking. Metacognitive questions embedded in the task can help them do just that. Traditionally, teachers tend to ask reflective questions at the end of a complex task, which does help students develop the useful habit of post hoc analysis. But metacognition should also occur *during* a task.

Rick Greenfield, a seventh-grade math teacher, wants to encourage his students' development of metacognition. Before the learners begin an independent task, he reminds them to think through the problems as they work, using four questions designed by Anderson (2002):

1. **What am I trying to accomplish?** This first question encourages students to locate the purpose. In this case, it causes his learners to think about what the equation is asking of them.

2. **What strategies am I using?** The second question requires students to determine what will be required of them, such as converting an improper fraction in order to solve for an unknown.

3. **How well am I using the strategies?** Students need to monitor a complex task in order to see if it is working, which means they must pause to see if they are headed in the right direction. The ability to make a midcourse correction is an important factor in developing procedural knowledge. Mr. Greenfield promotes this by setting a two-minute timer to remind students to stop and evaluate their progress.

Teachers need to aim for three quality indicators that deepen learning in the independent phase of instruction.

4. **What else could I do?** We expect students to get stuck; if that doesn't occur from time to time, then the work is too easy. But we also need to promote resilience and flexible thinking. This last question reminds Mr. Greenfield's students that thinking mathematically involves reasoning and exploring alternative solutions.

Mr. Greenfield reports that this process works well in his classroom. He explains, "The mathematical practices call for them to 'make sense of problems and persevere in solving them.' I tell them that the solution to the problem isn't going to announce itself: 'Hey, here's how to solve me!' They have to actively dig around for it, try different approaches, and really wrestle with it. These metacognitive questions are posted in my room, they are modeled regularly by me, and they are at the top of every worksheet they handle. I told them from the first day that math is muscular, and we're math warriors."

Self-awareness about learning evolves over a lifetime.

Does It Promote Goal Setting?

A second quality indicator concerns goal setting by the student. Learners should understand how goal setting advances their goals, as this is the basis of intrinsic motivation. Students' motivators vary, but they are likely to include some mix of performance (grades and recognition), mastery (acquiring knowledge), and work-avoidant (conserving effort) goals (Alexander & Jetton, 2000).

While the phrase "work-avoidant" may not sound like something positive, effort, outcome, and efficiency are things that all of us consider in our own decisions. For example, we may weigh an opportunity by thinking about the possible reward and the chance to advance our learning, but we always consider the benefits within the context of the amount of effort it will require to achieve them. Students are no different.

High school English teacher Robin Alexander builds goal setting into her students' assignments for written essays and research papers. These tasks require quite a bit of effort, but there are performance and mastery elements at stake as well. After discussing the writing project at hand, she asks each student to set a performance goal (the grade they want to achieve), a mastery goal (what they propose to learn during the process), and their planned effort (how many hours they will invest). They submit their goals to her in advance, and she uses these during writing conferences. When students submit the assignment, they also rate themselves on the attainment of their goals: the expected grade, the evidence

CHAPTER 5

of achievement of the learning goal, and the amount of time they actually spent on the assignment.

Ms. Alexander finds this approach works very well. "I have found these to be among the most valuable conversations I've had this year," she says. "Conferences about their progress toward their goals can jumpstart a less-than-diligent student. And when it comes to grading, they can see how their efforts played an active role in the result."

Does It Promote Self-Regulation?

A third indicator for independent learning concerns the ability to assume autonomy and develop a sense of efficacy. Self-regulation doesn't stand apart from the first two quality indicators; in fact, metacognition and goal setting are necessary in order to self-regulate learning.

Choice is critical for developing a sense of autonomy. Independent learning tasks should not be "anything goes," freewheeling assignments, but students should have the freedom to explore and customize their learning. As one example, teachers can use independent reading assignments to prompt students to develop the principles of self-regulation. When teachers present learners with all the reading material up front, along with a list of deadlines, instead of assigning the material as individual assignments in smaller chunks and stating, "Read this for tomorrow," then students get the opportunity to formulate their own reading plan.

A final aspect of self-regulation involves providing students with opportunities to explore and expand their own learning. As an example, high school biology teacher Lauren Oldfield introduces possible subjects for the science of natural selection and adaptation research papers her students will develop, but then lets them choose which topic to pursue.

"I give them options for them to choose from, like sexual selection, camouflage, and mimicry," she explains. "One student got very involved with the panda's thumb after reading an essay by Stephen Jay Gould. Another looked at some recent research about the development of human male hands to fight. They converted their research into short videos, which they posted for one another on our learning management system. I think having a forum to share their research was as important for them as the research itself. Everyone needs an audience."

Conclusion

Multilingual learners benefit from a robust instructional framework that aligns with what the educational sciences tell us about learning. That

> Learners should understand how goal setting advances their goals, as this is the basis of intrinsic motivation.

CHAPTER 5

means we must weave language and linguistic supports into our content instruction. Students benefit from focused instruction that incorporates teacher clarity practices with direct instruction, teacher modeling, and demonstration. However, students must also have opportunities to produce language that requires them to use critical-thinking skills in the company of others and to access complex texts. Teachers create access to complex texts and concepts by ensuring that linguistic and knowledge demands are addressed. And while all students can benefit from independent learning opportunities, those opportunities must be designed as thoughtfully as other aspects of instruction. Solid independent learning encourages goal setting, metacognition, and self-regulation.

Checks Into Learning

6

Big Idea

Classroom assessments should be used to monitor the progress of multilingual learners' development of content knowledge and language skills; they should also be used to plan future instruction.

Questions Educators Ask

- What are the purposes and uses of assessment when it comes to multilingual learners?

- How can we implement an assessment system that yields useful results?

- What types of data can be collected to monitor students' progress?

- How can we teach students how to interpret their data to make sense of where they need to go next in their learning?

Let's pause for a minute and take a test. Are you nervous? Do you think people will judge you because of your answers? Let's begin.

Intelligence Test Instructions

Write down each answer. It makes a difference! You will be allowed 10 minutes to complete the test. Write your answers in the spaces provided. Are you ready? What is the time? Start.

1. Some months have 30 days, some months have 31 days. How many months have 28 days?

   _____

2. If a doctor gives you 3 pills and tells you to take 1 pill every half hour, how long would it be before all the pills have been taken?

   _____

3. I went to bed at 8 o'clock in the evening, wound up my clock, and set the alarm to sound at 9 o'clock in the morning. How many hours of sleep would I get before being awoken by the alarm?

   _____

4. Divide 30 by half and add 10. What do you get?

   _____

5. A farmer had 17 sheep. All but 9 died. How many live sheep were left?

   _____

6. If you had only one match and entered a *cold* and *dark* room, with an oil heater, an oil lamp, and a candle, which would you light first?

   _____

7. A man builds a house with 4 sides of rectangular construction, each side having a southern exposure. A big bear comes along. What color is the bear?

   _____

8. Take 2 apples from 3 apples. What do you have?

   _____

9. How many animals of each species did Moses take with him on the Ark?

   _____

10. Suppose you drove a bus from Chicago with 43 people on board and stopped at Pittsburgh to pick up 7 more people and drop off 5 passengers and stopped at Cleveland to drop off 8 passengers and pick up 4 more and eventually arrived at Philadelphia 20 hours later. What's the name of the driver?

    _____

The answers to this test are found on page 97 at the end of the chapter. How did you do? How do you feel about your performance? Is there anything that you could do differently next time you take a test like this? Did you want to complain about the bias in some of these items? Do you think your results are representative of your skills?

Informing Instruction

The results of standardized tests are commonly used to allocate resources, determine which students need intervention, identify "failing" schools, and decide whether a student may graduate from high school. In this climate of accountability, testing assumes an increasingly important role in the curriculum structure and in the amount of instructional time dedicated to it. Yet the efficacy of any single assessment to determine such a wide scope of variables seems unlikely.

Although there may be a tendency to overgeneralize what test scores can reveal, assessment purposes extend beyond the single dimension of testing large numbers of students to provide broad measures of group achievement. There are a number of different reasons to assess students' learning, including

- Diagnosing an individual student's needs and making decisions regarding placement

- Diagnosis of progress speed and direction toward the success criteria

- Providing accountability information

- Evaluating programs

- Informing instruction

The last purpose, informing instruction, serves as the focus of this chapter. In an era in which the broadly collected data from standardized tests are being used to make far-reaching educational decisions about large groups of students, it is important that classroom assessments also be recognized for their contribution to what is known about an individual student.

Classroom assessments are those selected and administered by the teacher to determine what instruction needs to occur next. Assessments can be either formal or informal. Figures 6.1 and 6.2 provide information about the types of assessments teachers use.

Astute classroom teachers possess a wealth of information about their students' knowledge of literacy, language, and content, and they evaluate students' performance to gauge progress and guide future instruction. Wise practitioners recognize the value of such assessments as a rich source of data.

FIGURE 6.1 Formal Assessments		
TYPE	PURPOSE	ADMINISTRATION
Standardized, Norm-Referenced	Yields a student's academic performance ranking compared to a normed sample of students	• Schedule; determined by state and local agencies; often yearly • Tests are usually timed and have strict protocols
Standardized, Criterion-Referenced	Measures a student's performance compared to a set of academic skills or objectives. Scores are reported as the proportion of correct answers	• Rests may be timed or untimed • May be administered annually or more frequently

CHAPTER 6

FIGURE 6.2 Informal Assessments		
TYPE	**PURPOSE**	**ADMINISTRATION**
Observation	Gathers information about a student's academic, behavioral, or social skills used in an authentic setting	Teacher records observational data in anecdotal notes, journals, or daily logs
Portfolio	Provides evidence of a student's academic growth through the collection of work samples	Student and teacher select representative samples of student work for display in a binder or other organizer
Inventory	Documents student's use of specified skills during a single observation	A commercially or teacher-produced form of observable behaviors is completed by the teacher
Conference	Involves the student in direct feedback to the teacher in a one-to-one discussion	Often scheduled by the teacher at regular intervals to gauge progress on more complex academic behaviors such as reading comprehension
Self-Assessment	Allows the student to engage in reflective learning and think about learning	Students assess their own academic performance using an age-appropriate checklist of indicators
Survey	Collects student feedback about interests, prior knowledge, or motivation about a topic	Student completes a commercially or teacher-produced survey of items

Implementing an Assessment System

Calfee and Hiebert (1991) proposed that teachers participate in three phases of teacher-based assessment: *setting goals and purposes, collecting data,* and *interpretation.* In this model, assessment is infused into instruction rather than seen as something separate from the instructional flow of the classroom (e.g., Fisher & Frey, 2014). It is the interpretation phase that turns out the most powerful (provided the first two phases are correct) and if no interpretation, then there is less value. Where there is interpretation, there is meaning and traction. Let's look at each component in more detail.

Setting Goals and Purposes of Gathering Assessment Data

The teacher's beliefs influence the goals and purposes of gathering assessment data about what constitutes learning, the frequency and timing of the administration of assessment tools, and the type of information needed by the teacher. When these goals and purposes closely match the students, the link between assessment and instruction becomes clear-cut and definitive. However, when the goals and purposes do not complement the instruction, educators and learners struggle to find meaning in these time-consuming practices. In fact, when teachers protest that they "do not have time" to assess, it may actually be an instance of a poor match of assessments to students.

One of the strongest predictors of teachers' choices of assessment tools is the way those educators define language, literacy, and learning. In a classroom where teachers highly value responses to literature, much of the assessment will likely focus on reflection and literature circle discussions. In contrast, teachers who emphasize fluency and automaticity arc might use measures of words read per minute. In a classroom where content reigns supreme, assessments will likely be void of language-related items. Educators often have an easier time linking assessment to instruction when a menu of tools is available to match their classroom practice.

When and where an assessment is given also reflects the teacher's goals and purposes. For example, even the most carefully designed assessments are squandered if they are used infrequently and erratically. To avoid this, many teachers check for understanding at regular intervals to make instructional decisions that respond to current student needs.

Like frequency, the timing of the assessment also reveals the teacher's goals. Some choose an anticipatory activity at the beginning of a lesson to provide information about the content to be taught. One example of this is the KWL chart (Ogle, 1986), which asks students to identify what they *know*, what they *want to know,* and, later, what they have *learned*. Analysis of student responses on a KWL chart can alert the teacher to the specific background knowledge or vocabulary that needs to be taught, as well as those elements that require only a brief review.

As an example, let's look at Natasha Alexander's fifth-grade class, which is creating a KWL chart to correspond with their focus on illusions. This activity is done in preparation for a two-week unit on the relationship between the eye and the brain.

To begin, the teacher asks the students, "What do you already know about illusions?"

"Those magic eye paintings are illusions!" Arian calls out, gesturing to the posters on the table at the back of the room.

Patrick chimes in, saying, "Magicians perform illusions."

Ms. Alexander takes notes as her students continue to discuss what they know and what they want to know. Figure 6.3 contains the information she collects, which guides her decisions about targeted vocabulary and needed background information. She is also able to plan small-group lessons based on the data. At the end of the unit, small groups of students will complete the final column, "What have we learned?"

FIGURE 6.3 KWL Chart		
WHAT DO WE KNOW ABOUT ILLUSIONS?	**WHAT DO WE WANT TO KNOW?**	**WHAT HAVE WE LEARNED?**
• Magic eye paintings are illusions • Magicians do them • They play tricks on your brain • They are entertaining • There are optical illusions • Some illusions are used in art • Animals use illusion to hide (camouflage)	• Do they work on everybody? • Could we invent new ones? • What happens in your brain when you see an illusion? • Do your eyes get mixed up, or your brain? • Are there other illusions? • Why do some animals use camouflage and others don't? • Why don't humans use camouflage?	

As with teacher beliefs, frequency, and timing, the type of information needed by the teacher also influences the selection of assessments. Teachers of emergent multilingual readers may choose assessments that yield a current analysis of each student's literacy skills so they can effectively instruct on problem-solving strategies such as chunking smaller word parts and blending sounds through the word. Teachers of more fluent multilingual readers may be concerned with their students' comprehension strategies. Vocabulary assessments, information webs, and extended writing responses are likely to be more common in these classrooms.

Collecting Data

After determining the goals and purposes of classroom assessments, teachers collect the information they seek about their students. Here are a few of the common ways teachers do this:

- Asking questions

- Collecting written responses

- Listening to students as they respond orally

- Using tools such as rubrics, checklists, or quizzes

Importantly, teachers who want to maintain the rigor of the lesson while supporting student learning should ensure that they collect data and check for understanding frequently throughout the lesson, approximately every five to ten minutes. There are literally hundreds of ways to collect data from students, and we'll highlight a few of them here.

Oral Language

One effective way to check for understanding is through oral language: speaking and listening. When students are doing the talking, the teacher has a chance to assess their understanding. There are several classroom structures that provide multilingual students an opportunity to talk, including think-pair-share, reciprocal teaching, literacy circles, discussion prompts, and Socratic seminars.

In addition to listening as learners interact, teachers can ask for retellings, which are a valuable way to check for understanding because they provide a glimpse into student thinking. For example, Jack Bradford, a sixth-grade science teacher, asks Celia, a multilingual learner, to retell a section of a video clip they have seen related to glacier formation and movement.

As part of her retelling, Celia says, "The glaciers take a long time to grow. Well, really they grow, like something alive, even though they are not alive. They grow when it snows and the snow pile together. It changes to this special kind of ice. But before that, there is this in-between ice called *firn*."

This retelling lets Mr. Bradford know that much of his teaching has stuck and that Celia is well on her way to understanding glaciers. In addition to content knowledge, teachers of multilingual learners pay attention to language development and collect evidence of how language is being used as well as the next steps for instruction.

Teachers who want to maintain the rigor of the lesson while supporting student learning should collect data and check for understanding frequently.

A commonly used assessment for planning instruction for multilingual learners is based on observing a student's oral language proficiency. The Student Oral Language Observation Matrix (SOLOM) is designed to inform teachers about students' strengths and weaknesses in oral English. The SOLOM, which is designed to assess authentic oral language used for real day-to-day classroom purposes and activities, can be found in the appendix. A study on the use of SOLOM demonstrated that the tool has "strong internal consistency reliability with criterion-related validity in the low to moderately correlated range" and the researchers suggest that it is a useful tool for informal assessment (Dennis et al., 2019, p. 65). There are other tools that educators can pay to use to assess the oral language of multilingual learners (e.g., Test of Language Development; Newcomer & Hammil, 2019).

To ensure that the SOLOM is as useful as possible, observe the student in several authentic classroom activities in which they interact with you and/or classmates, such as a cooperative group task. Each observation should last for about five minutes. On each occasion, mark the rankings on the matrix according to your impressions of the child's use of English. You may also wish to audio-record one or more of your sessions to go back and confirm your impressions or to look for certain patterns of errors or usage.

The SOLOM yields ratings for English language proficiency:

- Beginning/Entering = 0–5

- Early Intermediate/Beginning = 6–10

- Intermediate/Developing = 11–15

- Early Advanced/Expanding = 16–20

- Advanced/Bridging = 21–25

Using the SOLOM, Carla Fernandez, a third-grade teacher, assesses an eight-year-old student, Patrick, collecting data on three different occasions, including two academic settings and one social setting. Patrick came to the United States from the Philippines, where he received minimal instruction in English at school, and he has been enrolled in U.S. schools for just under two years.

During the assessment, Ms. Fernandez notes that Patrick's oral language proficiency is consistent in both social and academic settings. Out of the five traits, Patrick is strongest in comprehension. However, he needs further instruction and development in fluency, vocabulary, pronunciation, and grammar. For example, when she asks him about what he has read in a reading passage titled *Bruno*, Patrick replies, "About one boy with six years old has a dog his older now so about building dog house."

Overall, Patrick gains comprehensible input from academic instruction, but some things have to be repeated. Patrick is strong in math and in social studies, and he needs explicit instruction with grammar and pronunciation.

Based on the data obtained from the SOLOM, Ms. Fernandez plans to focus on new vocabulary words each day and have Patrick add them to his personal dictionary. To improve Patrick's fluency, she plans to have him do repeated readings, pair him up with a buddy for buddy reading, and have him participate in Reader's Theater. Overall, she concludes that one-on-one instruction, exposure to and instruction in standard English language usage, positive intervention, and fluency activities will help Patrick move into the higher stages of language proficiency.

Questioning

Questioning, which can be done orally or in writing, is the most common way teachers check for understanding. Unfortunately, not all questions are worthy of instructional time. To be useful, the initial questions teachers ask should be planned in advance. Of course, additional questions that probe student understanding will come to mind during the interactions teachers have with students, but these initial questions form the expectations for student understanding.

> To be useful, the initial questions teachers ask should be planned in advance.

Less helpful questions are those we like to call "guess what's in the teacher's head." More formally known as Initiate-Respond-Evaluate, or IRE (Cazden, 2001), this cycle privileges students who are willing to play the game. For example, let's say the math teacher asks, "When do we use the FOIL rule?" Three or four students raise their hands, and the teacher selects Tanya to respond. Tanya says, "When you multiply binomials," to which the teacher responds, "Good." IRE is typically used with recall information and provides only a few students an opportunity to respond.

Instead, quality checking for understanding suggests that teachers must ask questions requiring more complex and critical thinking; these questions should also be presented in a way that ensures many students need to respond. Several instructional routines provide students with practice in questioning habits, such as ReQuest (Manzo, 1969), in which students read with a partner and take turns asking and answering questions. As they practice, their teacher analyzes the types of questions they are asking and the appropriateness of the answers. Over time (and with instruction and practice), students tire of the literal and recall questions and move toward more interesting questions that require synthesis and evaluation.

Another way to question in an inclusive way is through audience response systems. These can be as basic as three-by-five-inch cards with answers on them that all students hold up to answer a question; in contrast, they can be as complex as handheld devices that allow each student to key in a response to a question. An online version of audience response systems that rely on text messages from smartphones can be found at www.polleverywhere.com.

Another way to question in an inclusive way is through audience response systems.

As an example of the use of basic cards, as part of their opinionnaire in biology, the teacher, Ms. Oldfield, provided students with a green card marked *Yes* and a red card marked *No*. As she read each statement about the ecosystem, students held up one of their cards to indicate if they agreed or disagreed. Given that they were red or green, she could quickly assess students' thinking. Her question about the impact of cleaning agents entering the water system through storm drains split the class, which provided her with information about where to focus the lesson.

Writing

When students are writing, they are thinking. In fact, it's nearly impossible to write and *not* think. That's why short writing-to-learn prompts are so effective for checking for understanding.

Teachers should develop or select prompts that are set up to provide them with information about student understanding. We are particularly taken with the RAFT writing prompt (Santa & Havens, 1995), which requires that students consider the *role, audience, format,* and *topic* in their writing. There are, of course, many other writing prompts that can be used, but RAFT is flexible and teaches perspective. For example, after conservation efforts during middle school science, Matthew Rincon asks his students to respond to the following RAFT:

  R Role = county environmentalist

  A Audience = board of supervisors

  F Format = report

  T Topic = five recommendations to improve conservation efforts

Similarly, while students in eighth-grade social studies are learning about the Gettysburg Address and the role that this speech had in shaping U.S. policy, Tina Ly asks her students to respond to the following RAFT:

CHAPTER 6

R   Role = person attending the Gettysburg dedication

A   Audience = family member

F   Format = personal letter

T   Topic = Lincoln's message

For younger students, teachers can use interactive writing charts (Fisher & Frey, 2018). This instructional tool calls for the teacher and students to begin by discussing the purpose and content of what is to be written. They then "share the pen" as the teacher facilitates the group's writing on chart paper, assisting the students in letter formation; letter-sound relationships; cumulative word analysis; and concepts about print, syntax, and semantics. Teachers can use student observation sheets to record important data for later analysis and instruction (see Figure 6.4).

For example, Jacob Klein has identified four students for observational data collection. He will be noting the progress of Luis,

FIGURE 6.4   Interactive Writing Observation Checklist

Student: _____ Date: _____

Writing Topic: _____

	PROFICIENT	ATTEMPTED	NOT EVIDENCED	NOT AVAILABLE
Letter formations (Record letters)				
Concepts of print				
Spacing				
Directionality				
Capitals				
Oral language				
Uses language to represent ideas				
Grammatically correct				
Predicts and recalls				
Uses accurate vocabulary				
Interacts with peers				
On topic				

Vu, Kelly, and Mubarek in three areas: oral language development, print conventions, and letter formation. Specifically, he will note evidence of the extent of their oral language skills during the group discussion of Mr. Klein's secret: A surprise guest will be arriving the next day to answer questions about the new aquarium in the classroom. The teacher's goal for this activity is to capture the students' questions about the fish in the tank, and their care and feeding. The students will use this class chart to guide their discussion the following day.

As Mr. Klein leads this interactive writing session, he notes whether Vu's contributions to the discussion are on topic. When Kelly is called to the chart to write, the teacher observes the student's use of spacing and other print conventions. Mr. Klein requires all the children to write the message on their whiteboards at the same time it is being recorded on the chart. Not only does this keep students engaged, but it also allows him to assess Luis's letter formations when he proudly holds up his whiteboard.

Mubarek, who arrived from Yemen only two weeks earlier, is just now beginning to participate in the classroom routines. Mr. Klein notes Mubarek's use of language to negotiate the sharing of the marker and whiteboard with his partner.

A more specific and diagnostic assessment for multilingual learners in the area of writing is analytic writing (McMaster & Espin, 2007). This tool assesses a student's progress across a number of features during a short (six- to ten-minute) writing sample:

- Total words written (TWW)

- Average number of words written per minute (AWPM)

- Total words spelled correctly (TWSC)

- Total number of complete sentences (TCS)

- Average length of complete sentences (ALCS)

- Correct punctuation marks (CPM)

- Correct word sequences (CWS)

- Incorrect word sequences (ICWS)

Teachers can administer the writing prompt to a group of students, and while the individual scoring can be labor intensive, students can participate in the scoring by counting the total words written (TWW) and the average number of words written per minute (AWPM). The other elements require a more skilled eye, especially the correct and incorrect word sequences. This feature is the number of times two adjacent words are used correctly in terms of spelling, grammar, capitalization, and context. Word sequences include the last word in one sentence and the first word in the next. Because of the qualitative nature of the results, it is easy to gauge the relative progress of a student participating in intervention.

Most of these indicators are self-explanatory, but word sequences deserve further elaboration. A word sequence is two adjacent words in a sentence that are spelled and capitalized correctly, and that makes sense within the context of the writing. On paper, a correct sequence is indicated by an upward-facing caret (^) and an incorrect one is marked with a downward-facing caret below the sentence line (ᵥ).

Third-grade student Yazmin was given six minutes to write a response to the following story starter: *Describe your favorite room in your house. Tell what is in there and why it is your favorite. Use the descriptive language we have been studying.* Here are the scored results.

> ^My^bathroom^is‚ovor‚the^house^. ^My^dog‚in‚kitchen^.
> ^I^am‚sleep^in‚bedroom^. ^My^sister‚watch‚his‚oclock‚.
> ^I^play‚my^friend^.

An analysis of her writing shows the following:

- Total words written (TWW): 24

- Average number of words written per minute (AWPM): 4

- Total words spelled correctly (TWSC): 21

- Total number of complete sentences (TCS): 5

- Average length of complete sentences (ALCS): 4.8

- Correct punctuation marks (CPM): 5/5

- Correct word sequences (CWS): 18

- Incorrect word sequences (ICWS): 11

- CWS – ICWS = 7

The results indicate that her overall writing fluency is low, averaging only four words per minute, and her sentences are equally short in length, demonstrating a lack of descriptive language or complex sentence structures. She uses punctuation correctly, although it is notable that only periods are needed. She starts all sentences with a capital letter, and she spells 87.5 percent of the words correctly. In addition to these strengths, there are a number of patterns that can be observed that will need additional instruction such as vocabulary development and syntactic rules that may be transferred from another language.

Tests

Although tests are typically considered tools used for grading, they can also be used to check for understanding and inform instruction. Incorrect answers on a test provide teachers with information about what students still need to learn. Tests can be developed in a number of different formats, ranging from multiple choice to dichotomous choice (true/false, yes/no, agree/disagree) to essays.

Here's an example of a true/false question: "As a star ages, its internal composition changes as nuclear reactions in its core convert one element into another." If only 60 percent of the students answer incorrectly, then this result informs their teacher that they are confused about some aspect of the life cycle of stars.

Stephen Robertson, a middle school science teacher, wants to know what his students have learned from their study of electricity. Language development is important to Mr. Robertson; he uses several language assessments, including the SOLOM, to plan his instruction. In addition, as a content teacher, he wants to assess students' mastery of the content. Therefore, the type of assessment he selects is based on the purpose of the assessment.

Given his goal of assessing content knowledge, Mr. Robertson plans a multiple-choice test that includes a writing prompt. On a specific day, the entire class takes the test. However, Mr. Robertson knows that he has to scaffold the test items for his multilingual learners. One of the questions from the test and the version that he modifies for a student with developing proficiency can be found in Figure 6.5.

Although tests are typically considered tools used for grading, they can also be used to check for understanding and inform instruction.

CHAPTER 6

FIGURE 6.5   Seventh-Grade Science Test

ORIGINAL ITEM

8. Suppose you were performing experiments to determine some properties of an electromagnet. You had available several batteries, a switch, a compass, several washers, a nail, and a long piece of wire that you could wrap around the nail in a coil. Which one of the following would likely **not** be an experimental conclusion?

   A. The greater the number of batteries added to the circuit, the greater the number of washers the electromagnet would be able to lift.

   B. If the two wires connected to the positive and negative ends of the battery were reversed, the compass needle would deflect (rotate) in the opposite direction.

   C. If additional turns of wire were wrapped around the nail, the strength of the electromagnet would increase.

   D. If the tip of the nail were moved closer and closer to the compass, the compass needle would deflect (rotate) less and less.

SCAFFOLDED ITEM

8. You will perform experiments to determine the properties of an electromagnet.

   Materials

   - Batteries
   - Switch
   - Compass
   - Several washers
   - Nail
   - Long piece of wire to wrap around the nail

   Which of the following would be an experimental conclusion?

   A. An electromagnet with more batteries lifts more washers.

   B. The compass needle rotates in the opposite direction when you reverse the wires connected to the positive and negative ends of the battery.

   C. The strength of the electromagnet increases when you wrap more wire around the nail.

   D. The compass needle rotates less when you move the nail closer to the compass.

As this example shows, the scaffolded item is restructured visually, the number of words is reduced, and that information is presented in such a way that students' content knowledge is required while the language demands are reduced.

Figure 6.6 provides a list of content assessment examples and strategies teachers can use to scaffold the assessment for multilingual learners.

FIGURE 6.6   Scaffolding Assessments

ASSESSMENT EXAMPLES	WITHOUT SCAFFOLDING	WITH SCAFFOLDING
Define/describe an object or concept.	Write a description of the object or concept and label it.	Write a *list* of the main features of the concept, or provide labels for objects in a *picture* that is *provided.*
Provide examples of a concept and justify them.	Provide three examples and explain orally or in writing why these are good examples.	*Select* three examples from a *list provided* and explain *orally* why they were selected.
Retell or summarize a text.	Write five main ideas from an article and give examples.	Complete an *outline* or a *semantic map.*
Write a word problem.	Create a problem from your own numbers; give an equation, story, and question.	Complete a word problem *given examples* and *an outline* of a sample problem.
Summarize a science experiment.	Write a summary of procedures in a science experiment following scientific principles.	*Complete* a summary *given a list* of procedures in science experiments, including questions, materials, a plan, observations, and conclusions, or *demonstrate* the steps using actual materials.

Source: Adapted from O'Malley and Valdez Pierce (1996, Figure 7.1).

Validity, like reliability, must be considered with all forms of assessments.

Interpreting Data

As noted earlier, it is virtually impossible to separate the phases of classroom assessment when it is done effectively because its recursive nature propels it in a fluid fashion: setting goals, collecting data, implementing interpretation and instruction, then setting new goals. There are, however, critical features of interpretation that teachers must consider.

One is the reliability of the information gathered. On any given day, a student may be able to perform (or fail to perform) a specific skill or task. A single performance may not indicate whether the skills have been mastered. To ensure that assessments are reliable, teachers should collect data on a regular basis. For example, Mr. Klein, the teacher shown earlier who is engaged with interactive writing, does not limit his data collection to a single event or to his observations only. In addition to the interactive writing, he has assessments of his students' letter recognition skills, phonemic awareness, and developing phonics knowledge.

Validity, like reliability, must be considered with all forms of assessments. A way to increase validity in classroom assessment is to ensure that assessment reflects the daily instructional climate and does not require students to perform artificial tasks. For example, when Ms. Ly's class is focused on the Gettysburg Address, her assessment of their knowledge, both in terms of content and language, is based on the learning that they are doing. In this way, Ms. Ly can adjust lessons to address the needs of her students. Similarly, Mr. Bradford can respond in real time to his student's retelling because it is based on the content they are learning at that time.

Effective Assessment Practices

Assessments are often criticized when they replace instruction time. Teachers who understand the use of assessments as instructional tools do not need to take away valuable time to conduct assessments. Instead, they use their daily teaching events to collect data, as we've profiled in this chapter. The key is understanding which student will be the focus of assessment data collection for the day and which tools will produce the best, or most useful, information. Here's how teachers can ensure this occurs.

Match Assessments With Instructional Practice

Teachers must select tools that provide them with useful information. It would not be helpful for Mr. Klein to use a KWL chart during interactive writing, even though KWL charts provide useful information in the right context. Different assessment tools have different purposes and yield different information.

Use a Variety of Tools

No single assessment tool can provide all the information teachers need to plan instruction. When teachers use a variety of assessment tools, they allow multilingual learners to demonstrate their understanding in ways that do not require language skills they have not yet acquired. The composite view provided by these various assessment tools allows teachers to generalize student learning and required instruction.

Plan Instruction After Assessment

All too often, teachers plan their instruction and then determine the assessments they will use to gauge students' success and determine student progress. Wise teachers know what each student needs to be taught next, and they plan learning events that allow the student to accomplish that task. As the teachers plan, they are also aware of opportunities to gather additional assessment information about students to make midcourse corrections. These teachers focus on what students already know and can do as the basis for instructional planning, which is known as asset-based or strengths-based instruction.

Make Assessment Recursive

The most important lesson we have learned from teachers of multilingual learners is that the link between assessment and instruction is not linear. The teachers profiled in this chapter understand the recursive nature of setting goals and purposes and of collecting and interpreting data. They know that this interpretation will result in the establishment of future learning goals, and it will direct new data collection that requires interpretation. Their classrooms illustrate how teaching and learning are parts of a continuous process in which teachers use information about student learning to plan their teaching.

> Wise teachers know what each student needs to be taught next, and they plan learning events that allow the student to accomplish that task.

Conclusion

Linking assessment and instruction is a central feature of effective teaching and learning. There are several tools that teachers can use to collect data, but without careful analysis, the data are not likely to impact students' learning. When classroom assessments are used to design learning experiences rather than to document learning exclusively, students benefit.

Answers to Opening Questions

1. All of them. Every month has at least 28 days.

2. 1 hour. If you take a pill at 1 o'clock, then another at 1:30, and the last at 2 o'clock, they will be taken in 1 hour.

3. 1 hour. It is a wind-up alarm dock, which cannot discriminate between AM and PM.

4. 70. Dividing by half is the same as multiplying by 2.

5. 9 live sheep.

6. The match.

7. White. If all walls face south, the home must be on the North Pole.

8. 2 apples, I have 3 apples, you take 2. What do you have?

9. None. It was Noah, not Moses.

10. YOU are the driver.

Final Thoughts

As we come to the of this book, we are reminded that teaching multilin-gual learners is both rewarding and challenging. We have presented the evidence for effective teaching and learning in five areas:

- Climate for learning

- Challenge as learning

- Clarity of learning

- Cohesion in learning

- Checks into learning

In reality, these are much more integrated and interdependent than a linear book allows us to share. We believe each of these is important in its own right and that they influence one another. We also know that together they foster language, literacy, and content learning. As a reminder, literacy is freedom's gatekeeper. We know that the more literate an individual is, the more capable they are of reaching their educational and career aspirations. After all, a major measure of effective schooling is the literacy attainment of its graduates. But the impact of literacy reaches far beyond classroom walls. Literate con-sumers can read rental agreements and challenge unfair housing prac-tices. Literate citizens can discern between real and fake news and question sources. Literate community members can use their voices to advocate on behalf of those who are marginalized. Literate members of a society are less vulnerable to being victimized by those who do not have their best interests at heart.

> Literacy is freedom's gatekeeper.

Among the most vulnerable in this country are those who are not fully literate in English. This limitation is a source of unintended, but very real institutional inequities. The conversational aspects of language acquisi-tion, which are primarily of a social nature, are important in everyday human interactions. Children and adolescents who are learning English as a subsequent language need to develop these skills and generally do so early on. But too many stalls when it comes to developing more formal academic reading and writing skills that match their critical-thinking skills. When these long-term English learners (LTEL) fail to advance in their acquisition of academic language, the result is a diminished level of independence. Instead, they are forced to remain dependent on others to make decisions that require a high degree of literacy. Progress for all multilingual learners must be accelerated. It's time to double down on our efforts by doubling up on our practices. We must all teach and lead with a sense of urgency (e.g., Soto, 2021). Identify high-impact approaches that accelerate student literacy learning and amplify teacher collaboration, and then apply them with a degree of frequency, intensity, and duration such that they can deliver on their promise. By doing so, we deliver on our promise for more equitable schools for all our students.

Appendix

Student Oral Language
Observation Matrix (SOLOM)

Student Name: _____ Grade: _____ Age: _____ Language: _____

	1	2	3	4	5	SCORES
Comprehension	Cannot be said to understand even simple conversation	Has great difficulty following what is said Comprehends only social conversation spoken slowly with frequent repetitions	Understands most of what is said at slower-than-normal speed with repetitions	Understands nearly everything at normal speed, although occasional repetition may be necessary	Understands everyday conversations and normal classroom discussions without difficulty	
Fluency	Speech is so halting and fragmentary as to make conversation virtually impossible	Usually hesitant; often forced into silence by language limitations	Speech in everyday conversation is somewhat limited because of inadequate vocabulary	Speech in everyday conversation and classroom discussion is generally fluent, with occasional lapses while the student searches for the correct manner of expression	Speech in everyday conversation and classroom discussion is fluent and effortless, approximating that of a native speaker	
Vocabulary	Vocabulary limitations are so extreme as to make conversation virtually impossible	Misuse of words and very limited vocabulary make comprehension quite difficult	Frequently uses the wrong words; conversation somewhat limited because of inadequate vocabulary	Occasionally uses inappropriate terms and/or must rephrase ideas because of lexical inadequacies	The use of vocabulary and idioms approximates that of a native speaker	

	1	2	3	4	5	SCORES
Pronunciation	Pronunciation problems are so severe as to make speech virtually unintelligible	Very hard to understand because of pronunciation problems Must frequently repeat in order to be understood	Pronunciation problems necessitate concentration on the listener's part and occasionally lead to misunderstanding	Always intelligible, though one is conscious of a definite accent and occasional inappropriate intonation patterns	Pronunciation and intonation approximate that of a native speaker	
Grammar	Errors in grammar and word order are so severe as to make speech virtually unintelligible	Grammar and word errors make comprehension difficult Must often rephrase and/or restrict self to basic patterns	Makes frequent errors of grammar and word order that occasionally obscure meaning	Occasionally makes grammatical and/or word order errors that do not obscure meaning	Grammatical usage and word order approximate that of a native speaker	
Stages of Language Development	Pre-Production Score: 20%	Early Production Score: 24–40%	Speech Emergence Score: 44–60%	Intermediate Score: 64–80%	Advanced Native-Like Fluency Score: 84–100%	**Total** ____ × 4 = ____ %

Source: California Department of Education.

References

Alexander, P. A., & Jetton, T. L. (2000). Learning from text: A multidimensional and developmental perspective. In M. L. Kamil, P. B. Mosenthal, P. D. Pearson, & R. Barr (Eds.), *Handbook of reading research* (Vol. III, pp. 285–310). Erlbaum.

Alter, P., & Haydon, T. (2017). Characteristics of effective classroom rules: A review of the literature. *Teacher Education & Special Education, 40*(2), 114–127.

Anderson, J. R., Fincham, J. M., & Douglass, S. A. (1999). Practice and retention: A unifying analysis. *Journal of Experimental Psychology: Learning, Memory, and Cognition, 25*, 1120–1136.

Anderson, N. J. (2002). The role of metacognition in second language teaching and learning. *Eric Clearinghouse on Language and Linguistics.* https://www.cal.org/publications/the-role-of-metacognition-in-second-language-teaching-and-learning/

August, D., & Shanahan, T. (2006). *Developing literacy in second-language learners: Report of the national literacy panel on language-minority children and youth.* Lawrence Erlbaum Associates.

Australia Children's Education and Care Quality Authority. (2018). Quality area 3: The environment and the 'third teacher'. *National Quality Standard Information Sheet.* https://www.acecqa.gov.au/sites/default/files/2018-04/QA3_TheEnvironmentAsTheThirdTeacher.pdf

Brown, B. (2018, October 15). *Clear is kind. Unclear is unkind.* https://brenebrown.com/articles/2018/10/15/clear-is-kind-unclear-is-unkind/

Buckingham, M. (2005). *The one thing you need to know.* Simon & Schuster.

Calfee, R. C., & Hiebert, E. H. (1991). Classroom assessment in reading. In R. Barr, M. Kamil, P. Rosenthal, & P. D. Pearson (Eds.), *Handbook of research on reading* (2nd ed., pp. 281–309). Longman.

California Department of Education. (2012). *California English language development standards, kindergarten through grade 12.* https://www.cde.ca.gov/sp/el/er/documents/eldstndspublication14.pdf

California Department of Education. (2021). *Initial ELPAC general performance level descriptors.* www.cde.ca.gov/ta/tg/ep/elpacipld.asp

Canillas, J. L. (2021). Teachers' perceptions of bilingualism: Toward a more equitable approach. *Thresholds in Education, 44*(1), 68–81.

Carter, E. W. (2021). Dimensions of belonging for individuals with intellectual and developmental disabilities. In J. L. Jones & K. L. Gallus (Eds.), *Belonging and resilience in individuals with developmental disabilities* (pp. 13–34). Springer. https://doi.org/10.1007/978-3-030-81277-5_2

Carter, E. W., & Biggs, E. E. (2021). *Creating communities of belonging for students with significant cognitive disabilities.* University of Minnesota, TIES Center.

CASEL. (2019). Sample lesson plan: Generating classroom shared agreements. *Guide to Schoolwide SEL.* https://schoolguide.casel.org/resource/sample-lesson-plan-generating-classroom-shared-agreements/

Casey, J. E. (2018). The effects of reciprocal teaching on Hispanic students' awareness of comprehension strategies for expository text. *Journal of the International Association of Special Education, 18*(1), 9–22.

Cazden, C. B. (2001). *Classroom discourse: The language of teaching and learning* (2nd ed.). Heinemann.

Cohen, J. (1988). *Statistical power analysis for the behavioral sciences* (2nd ed.). Erlbaum.

Coleman, J. S., Campbell, E. Q., Hobson, C. J., McPartland, J., Mood, A. M., Weinfeld, F. D., & York, R. L. (1966). *Equality of educational opportunity.* U.S. Government Printing Office.

Council of Great City Schools. (n.d.) *Juicy sentences play.* www.cgcs.org/cms/lib/ DC 00001581/Centricity/Domain/251/CGCS _GCS_Sentence%20Play_flyer_v5 .pdf

Cruickshank, D. R., & Kennedy, J. J. (1986). Teaching clarity. *Teaching and Teacher Education, 2*(1), 43–47.

Dennis, L. R., Krach, S. K., McCreery, M. P., & Navarro, S. (2019). The student oral language observation matrix: A psychometric study with preschoolers. *Assessment for Effective Intervention, 45*(1), 65–72.

Duckworth, A. (2016). *Grit: The power of passion and perseverance.* Scribner.

Dweck, C. S. (2006). *Mindset: The new psychology of success.* Ballantine.

Echevarria, J., Short, D., & Powers, K. (2006). School reform and standards-based education: A model for English-language learners. *Journal of Educational Research, 99*(4), 195–210.

Edmondson, A. (1999). Psychological safety and learning behavior in work teams. *Administrative Science Quarterly, 44*(2), 350–383.

Elliott, A. J., Fairchild, M. D., & Franklin, A. (Eds.) (2015). *The handbook of color psychology: Cambridge handbooks in psychology.* Cambridge University Press.

Emmer, E. T., Evertson, C. M., & Worsham, M. E. (2002). *Classroom management for secondary teachers* (6th ed.). Pearson Allyn & Bacon.

Fendick, F. (1990). *The correlation between teacher clarity of communication and student achievement gain: A meta-analysis* [Doctoral dissertation]. University of Florida Digital Collections. https://ufdc .ufl.edu/AA00032787/00001

Fenner, D. S., & Snyder, S. (2017). *Unlocking English learners' potential: Strategies for making content accessible.* Corwin.

Fillmore, L. W., & Fillmore, C. J. (n.d.). What does text complexity mean for English learners and language minority students? *Understanding Language Project.* Stanford University. https://ul.stanford .edu/sites/default/files/resource/2021-12/ 06-LWF%20CJF%20Text%20Complexity %20FINAL_0.pdf

Fisher, D., & Frey, N. (2010). Unpacking the language purpose: Vocabulary, structure, and function. *TESOL Journal, 1*(3), 315–337.

Fisher, D., & Frey, N. (2014). *Checking for understanding: Formative assessment techniques for your classroom* (2nd ed.). ASCD.

Fisher, D., & Frey, N. (2018). Write from the start. *Educational Leadership, 75*(7), 80–83.

Fisher, D., & Frey, N. (2021). *Better learning through structured teaching: a framework for the gradual release of responsibility* (3rd ed.). ASCD.

Fisher, D., & Frey, N. (2022). Tending to learning environments. *Educational Leadership, 80*(4), 74–75.

Fisher, D., Frey, N., & Hattie, J. (2016). *Visible learning for literacy, grades K–12: Implementing the practices that work best to accelerate student learning.* Corwin Literacy.

Fisher, D., Frey, N., & Rothenberg, C. (2011). *Implementing RTI with English learners.* Solution Tree.

Gámez, P. B., & Lesaux, N. K. (2012). The relation between exposure to sophisticated and complex language and early-adolescent English-only and language minority learners' vocabulary. *Child Development, 83*(4), 1316–1331.

García, O. (2020). Translanguaging and Latinx bilingual readers. *The Reading Teacher, 73*(5), 557–562.

Garrett, R., & Hong, G. (2016). Impacts of grouping and time on the math learning of language minority kindergartners. *Educational Evaluation and Policy Analysis, 38*, 222–244.

Gerena, L. (2011). Parental voice and involvement in cultural context: Understanding rationales, values, and motivational constructs in a dual immersion setting. *Urban Education, 46*(3), 342–370.

González-Howard, M., & Suárez, E. (2021). Retiring the term English language learners: Moving toward linguistic justice through asset-oriented framing. *Journal of Research in Science Teaching, 58*(5), 749–752.

Good, T. L. (1987). Two decades of research on teacher expectations: Findings and future directions. *Journal of Teacher Education, 38*(4), 32–47.

Gottlieb, M. (2021). *Classroom assessment in multiple languages: A handbook for teachers.* Corwin.

Hall, R. M., & Sandler, B. R. (1982). *The classroom climate: A chilly one for women?* Project on the Status and Education of Women, Association of American Colleges.

Halliday, M. A. K. (1976). Anti-languages. *American Anthropologist, 78*(3), 570–584.

Hattie, J. (2017, June 28). Misinterpreting the growth mindset: Why we're doing students a disservice. *Education Week.* www.edweek.org/education/opinion-misinterpreting-the-growth-mindset-why-were-doing-students-a-disservice/2017/06

Hattie, J. (2023). *Visible learning: The sequel.* Routledge.

Hattie, J., & Hattie, K. (2022). *10 steps to develop great learners: Visible Learning for parents.* Routledge.

Hill, J., & Flynn, K. (2006). *Classroom instruction that works with English language learners.* ASCD.

Hines, C. V., Cruickshank, D. R., & Kennedy, J. J. (1985). Teacher clarity and its relationship to student achievement and satisfaction. *American Educational Research Journal, 22*(1), 87–99.

Honigfeld, A. M., Dove, M. G., Cohan, A., & Goldman, C. M. (2021). *From equity insights to action: Critical strategies for teaching multilingual learners.* Corwin.

Keller, T. (2020). *When you trap a tiger.* Random House Children's Books.

Kline, R. B. (2004). *Beyond significance testing: Reforming data analysis methods in behavioral research.* American Psychological Association.

Krashen, S. D. (1986). *Principles and practice in second language acquisition.* Pergamon Press.

Lai, L., & Wang, R. (2016). The silent experience of young bilingual learners: A sociocultural study into the silent period. *International Journal of Bilingual Education & Bilingualism, 19*(3), 332–335.

Lewis, G., Jones, B., & Baker, C. (2012). Translanguaging: Origins and development from school to street and beyond. *Educational Research and Evaluation, 18*(7), 641–654.

Long, M. H. (1990). The least a second language acquisition theory needs to explain. *TESOL Quarterly, 24*(4), 649–666.

Manzo, A. V. (1969). The request procedure. *Journal of Reading, 13*(2), 123–126.

Martin, A. J., & Marsh, H. W. (2006). Academic resilience and its psychological and educational correlates: A construct validity approach. *Psychology in the Schools, 43*(3), 267–281.

Maslow, A. H. (1943). A theory of human motivation. *Psychological Review, 50*(4), 370–396. https://doi.org/10.1037/h0054346

McMaster, K., & Espin, C. (2007). Technical features of curriculum-based measurement in writing: A literature review. *Journal of Special Education, 40*(2), 68–84.

Mercer, N., & Wegerif, R. (2004). Is 'exploratory talk' productive talk? In H. Daniels & A. Edwards (Eds.), *The Routledge falmer reader in psychology of education* (pp. 67–86). Routledge Falmer.

Moll, L., Amanti, C., Neff, D., & González, N. (1992). Funds of knowledge for teaching: Using a qualitative approach to connect homes and classrooms. *Theory Into Practice, 31*(2), 132–141.

Morell, M., Yang, J. S., Gladstone, J. R., Turci Faust, L., Ponnock, A. R., Lim, H. J., & Wigfield, A. (2021). Grit: The long and short of it. *Journal of Educational Psychology, 113*(5), 1038–1058.

Morishima, Y. (2013). Allocation of limited cognitive resources during text comprehension in a second language. *Discourse Processes, 50*(8), 577–597.

Murphy, D. (2014). The academic achievement of English learners: Data for the US and each of the states. *Child Trends.* https://www.childtrends.org/wp-content/uploads/2015/07/2014-62Academic Achievement English.pdf

National Center for Education Statistics. (2022). English learners in public schools. *Condition of Education.* U.S. Department of Education, Institute of Education Sciences. https://nces.ed.gov/programs/coe/indicator/cgf

New York State Education Department, & Office of Bilingual Education and World Languages. (2019). *Multilingual learner/ English language learner graduation rate improvement and dropout prevention planning tool.* Author. www.nysed.gov/common/nysed/files/programs/bilingual-ed/ellmll-grad-and-dropout-toolkit_4_12_19_final.pdf

New York State Education Department. (2021). *NY State graduation rate data 4 year outcome as of August 2021.* Author. https://data.nysed.gov/gradrate.php?year=2021&state=yes

Newcomer, P. L., & Hammil, D. D. (2019). *Test of language development–Primary* (5th ed.). WPS.

Nora, J., & Echevarria, J. (2016). *No more low expectations for English learners.* Heinemann.

Ogle, D. M. (1986). K-W-L: A teaching model that develops active reading of expository text. *The Reading Teacher, 39,* 564–570.

O'Malley, M., & Valdez Pierce, L. (1996). *Authentic assessment for English language learners: Practical approaches for teachers.* Addison Wesley.

Ostrander, J., Melville, A., Bryan, J. K., & Letendre, J. (2018). Proposed modification of a school-wide bully prevention program to support all children. *Journal of School Violence, 17*(3), 367–380.

Paley, V. G. (1992). *You can't say you can't play.* Harvard University Press.

Palincsar, A. S., & Brown, A. (1984). Reciprocal teaching of comprehension-fostering and comprehension-monitoring activities. *Cognition and Instruction, 1*(2), 117–175.

Pearson, P. D., & Gallagher, G. (1983). The gradual release of responsibility model of instruction. *Contemporary Educational Psychology, 8,* 112–123.

Perkins-Gough, D. D., & Duckworth, A. A. (2013). The significance of GRIT. *Educational Leadership, 71*(1), 14–20.

Pit-ten Cate, I. M., & Glock, S. (2018). Teacher expectations concerning students with immigrant backgrounds or special educational needs. *Educational Research & Evaluation, 24*(3–5), 277–294.

Pratt-Johnson, Y. (2015). Stressors experienced by immigrant and other non-native English-speaking students in U.S. schools and their families. *Journal of Social Distress & the Homeless, 24*(3), 140–150.

Priniski, S. J., Hecht, C. A., & Harackiewicz, J. M. (2018). Making learning personally meaningful: A new framework for relevance research. *Journal of Experimental Education, 86*(1), 11–29.

Quaglia Institute. (2022). *Student voice: A decade of data.* https://www.quagliainstitute.org/uploads/legacy/Student_Voice_Grades_6-12_Decade_of_Data_Report.pdf

Rosenshine, B., & Furst, N. (1971). Research on teacher performance criteria. In B. O. Smith (Ed.), *Research in teacher education* (pp. 37–72). Prentice Hall.

Rubie-Davies, C. (2008). *Expecting success: Teacher beliefs and practices that enhance student outcomes.* Verlog, Dr. Muller.

Rubie-Davies, C. (2014). *Becoming a high expectation teacher: Raising the bar.* Routledge.

Rubie-Davies, C., Hattie, J., & Hamilton, R. (2006). Expecting the best for students: Teacher expectations and academic outcomes. *The British Journal of Educational Psychology, 76*, 429–444. https://doi.org/10.1348/000709905X53589.

Rubie-Davies, C. M., & Peterson, E. R. (2016). Relations between teachers' achievement, over- and underestimation, and students' beliefs for Māori and Pākehā students. *Contemporary Educational Psychology, 47*, 72–83.

Sacramento County Office of Education. (n.d.). *How your English learner student will learn English: The California English language development (CA ELD) standards, kindergarten–grade 12.* https://www.scoe.net/media/jqoluuja/parent_overview_eld.pdf

Santa, C., & Havens, L. (1995). *Creating independence through student-owned strategies: Project CRISS.* Kendall Hunt.

Saphier, J., Haley-Speca, M. A., & Gower, R. R. (2008). *The skillful teacher: Building your teaching skills.* Research for Better Teaching, Inc.

Sapon-Shevin, M. (1998). *Because we can change the world: A practical guide to building cooperative, inclusive classroom communities.* Allyn & Bacon.

Scarcella, R. (2000). *Accelerating academic English: A focus on the English learner.* Regents of the University of California.

Short, D. J., & Fitzsimmons, S. (2007). *Double the work: Challenges and solutions to acquiring language and academic literacy for adolescent English language learners. A report to Carnegie Corporation of New York.* Alliance for Excellent Education.

Simonds, C. J. (1997). Classroom understanding: An expanded notion of teacher clarity. *Communication Research Reports, 14*(3), 279–290.

Smith, D., Fisher, D., & Frey, N. (2021). *Removing labels, grades K–12: 40 techniques to disrupt negative expectations about students and schools.* Corwin.

Soto, I. (2021). *Shadowing multilingual learners* (2nd ed.). Corwin.

Student Achievement Partners. (n.d.). *Juicy sentence guidance.* https://achievethecore.org/content/upload/Juicy%20Sentence%20Guidance.pdf

Stutzman, B., & Lowenhaupt, R. (2022). At the intersection: Examining teacher and administrator perceptions of ELs and special education. *International Journal of Disability, Development & Education, 69*(3), 1047–1064.

Swain, M. (1985). Communicative competence: Some roles of comprehensible input and comprehensible output in its development. In S. Gass & C. Madden (Eds.), *Input in second language acquisition* (pp. 235–256). Newbury House.

Swain, M. (1995). *Three functions of output in second language learning.* Oxford University Press.

The Education Hub. (2018). *How to develop high expectation teaching.* https://theeducationhub.org.nz/how-to-develop-high-expectations-teaching/

TNTP. (2018). *The opportunity myth: What students can show us about how school is letting them down—and how to fix it.* Author.

TNTP. (2022). *Unlocking acceleration: How below grade-level work is holding students back in literacy.* Author. https://tntp.org/assets/documents/Unlocking_Acceleration_8.16.22.pdf

Tough, P. (2012). *How children succeed: Grit, curiosity, and the hidden power of character.* Houghton Mifflin Harcourt.

U.S. Department of Education. (n.d.). *Academic performance and outcomes for English learners.* www2.ed.gov/datastory/el-outcomes/index.html

van den Noort, M., Struys, E., Bosch, P., Jaswetz, L., Perriard, B., Yeo, S., Barisch, P., Vermeire, K., Lee, S. H., & Lim, S. (2019). Does the bilingual advantage in cognitive control exist and if so, what are its modulating factors? A systematic review. *Behavioral Sciences, 9*(3), 27. https://doi.org/10.3390/bs9030027

Veerman, G. J., & Denessen, E. (2021). Social cohesion in schools: A non-systematic review of its conceptualization and instruments. *Cogent Education, 8*(1). https://doi.org/10.1080/2331186X.2021.1940633

Vygotsky, L. S. (1978). *Mind and society: The development of higher mental processes.* Harvard University Press.

Wang, S., Rubie-Davies, C. M., & Meissel, K. (2018). A systematic review of the teacher expectation literature over the past 30 years. *Educational Research & Evaluation, 24*(3–5), 124–179.

Wang, S. H., Lang, N., Bunch, G. C., Basch, S., McHugh, S. R., Huitzilopochtli, S., & Callanan, M. (2021). Dismantling persistent deficit narratives about the language and literacy of culturally and linguistically minoritized children and youth: Counterpossibilities. *Frontiers in Education, 6,* 641796. https://doi.org/10.3389/feduc.2021.641796

Wassell, B. A., Hawrylak, M. F., & Scantlebury, K. (2017). Barriers, resources, frustrations, and empathy: Teachers' expectations for family involvement for Latino/a ELL students in urban STEM classrooms. *Urban Education, 52*(10), 1233–1254.

Wheeler, R. S., & Swords, R. (2006). *Codeswitching: Teaching standard English in urban classrooms.* National Council of Teachers of English.

WIDA. (2020). WIDA *English language development standards framework, 2020 edition: Kindergarten–grade 12.* Board of Regents of the University of Wisconsin System.

Wood, D., Bruner, J. S., & Ross, G. (1976). The role of tutoring in problem solving. *Journal of Child Psychology, Psychiatry, & Applied Disciplines, 17,* 89–100.

Zacarian, D. (2023). *Transforming schools for multilingual learners: A comprehensive guide for educators.* Corwin.

Zinn, J. (2016). The sociology of risk. In K. Korgen (Ed.), *The Cambridge handbook of sociology.* Cambridge University Press.

Index

Academic language, 1, 13, 63, 69, 71, 100
Accessibility, 23
Affective filters, 51
Alternate ranking, 28–29
Arawaks, 69–70
Assessment tools, 2, 81, 82–84, 87, 91–92, 94, 95, 96–97
Assets, 7, 9, 56, 97
Audience response systems, 89
Australia Children's Education, 23, 24
Automaticity, 37
Autonomy, 76

Belonging, 17–19, 30
Biases, 11, 26, 52, 81
Big Idea, 5, 17, 31, 45, 61, 79
Brain, 43, 59, 84
Bridging proficiency level, 16, 49
Buckingham, M., 45
Buddy pairs, 21, 88
Bullying, 26–27

California English Language Development Standards, 49
California language proficiency levels, 16
Care Quality Authority, 23, 24
Carter, E. W., 19–20
CASEL (Collaborative for Academic, Social, and Emotional Learning), 25
Chunks, 62, 69, 76
Clarity, 14, 45–47, 49, 51, 58–59, 61
Classroom agreements, 25
Classroom assessments, 82–83, 86, 95–97
Classroom cohesion, 18
Classroom rules, 25, 33
Climate, 4, 14, 17–30, 81, 99
Codeswitching, 65, 66

Cognitive task analysis, 38
Collaboration, 8–10
Collaborative for Academic, Social, and Emotional Learning (CASEL), 25
Collaborative learning, 28, 63, 70, 72
Complex tasks, 74
Complexity and difficulty quadrants, 36
Complexity, 9, 36–38, 55
Comprehension, 7, 39, 72, 87
Conferences, 11, 75–76, 83
Confidence, 45, 61
Connections, 16, 20, 42, 58–59
Content learning, 10, 13, 39, 49–50, 53, 71, 86, 93–94, 99
Content standards, 48, 50
Context, 50, 75, 92
Contrastive grammar analysis, 65–67
Conversation, 10, 76, 99
Critical-thinking skills, 77, 100
Cumulative talk, 71, 73

Deeper thinking, 36, 39
Deficit mindset, 1
Descriptive language, 92–93
Differentiation, 34
Difficulty and complexity quadrants, 36
Difficulty, 36–38
Direct instruction, 2, 63, 67, 77
Disputational talk, 71, 73
Disputes, 27
Dual language program, 12, 58
Dweck, C. S., 21, 41

Education, 2, 6
Effort management, 21
Emerging proficiency level, 16, 49

English Language Advisory
    Committee (ELAC), 65
English language arts, 48, 50
Equity, 8–9
Errors, 41, 63, 66, 87
Ethnicity, 10–11, 26
Exclusion, 26
Expanding proficiency level, 16, 49
Exploratory talk, 71

Failure, 32–33, 41
Feedback, 2, 4, 32, 39, 47, 52, 56, 58
Figurative language, 52
Fillmore, C. J., 68–69
Fillmore, L. W., 68–69
Fisher, D., 2, 23, 50, 53, 54, 62, 68, 83, 90
Fluency, 37–39, 84, 87, 93
Formal assessments, 82
Frames, 55, 73
Frey, N., 23, 40–41, 53, 54, 62, 68, 83, 90
Function, 10, 53, 55

Generations, 14
Goal setting, 34, 38, 75–77, 83–84, 95, 97
Grading, 76, 93
Gradual release of responsibility, 42, 62
Grammar, 53, 55, 63, 64, 65–67, 68, 87–88, 92
Grouping, 27–28
Growth mindset, 21, 41
Guided instruction, 67–68

Hattie, J., 2, 3, 12, 39, 41
Hattie, K., 12
Helping curriculum, 20–21
Heritage language, 9, 12, 21
High expectations, 32–35, 43
Home languages, 14, 38, 65–67
Homework, 11–12

Illusions, 84–85
Independent work, 2, 74, 76
Influences on learning, 3, 18
Informal assessments, 83
Informational text, 37, 39
Initiate-respond-evaluate (IRE), 88
Intelligence test, 80–81
Interactions, 13, 26, 33
Interactive writing checklist, 90
Interpretation, 83, 95, 97

Kindergarten, 28
Know, Want to Learn, Learned (KWL),
    84–85, 96

Language conventions, 53
Language frames, 55, 73
Language proficiency, 14, 16, 28,
    48, 70, 87–88, 91
Language purpose statements, 54
Language specialists, 9
Language structure, 68–69
Learning environment survey, 24
Learning environment, 12, 16–17, 51
Learning goals, 34, 47, 76, 97
Learning intentions and success criteria, 33,
    39, 46–48, 50–57, 59, 61, 81
Learning management system, 41, 76
Letter formations, 90–91
Listening, 15, 50, 56, 86
Literacy, 7, 68, 83–84, 99–100
Long-term English learners. *See* LTEL
Lower expectations, 11, 28, 33
LTEL (long-term English learners), 100

Maslow, A. H., 18
Maslow's hierarchy of needs, 19
Mastery, 18, 39, 75, 93
Mercer, N., 71
Meta-analyses, 3, 47
Metacognition, 74–77
Metalanguage, 68
Mistakes, 13, 15, 42–43, 66
Motivation, 15, 34, 51, 69
Music, 50

Name calling, 26
National Center for Education Statistics, 7
New York State Education Department, 8
Nouns, 49–50, 69

Open questions, 34
Opportunity to learn (OTL), 9
Optimism, 40, 45
Oral language, 49, 70, 86–87, 91
Oromo language, 66–67

Pairing students, 21, 27, 88
Pakistan, 5–6
Pandemic, 11

Paragraph frames, 55
Parent involvement, 11–12, 38, 65–67
Partnering, 21, 52, 71, 88, 91
Peace table, 27
Perseverance, 37, 40
Persistence, 6, 21, 40–42
Personal association, 58
Physical activity, 50
Poverty, 15
Print conventions, 91
Proficiency, 10–12, 14–16, 21, 49, 70–71
Proximity, 22–23
Public school statistics, 7

Quadrants, task complexity, 36–40
Quality indicators, 52, 74–76
Questions Educators Ask, 5, 17, 31, 45, 61, 79

RAFT (role, audience, format, topic), 89
Reciprocal teaching (RT), 62, 72–73, 86
Relevance, 3, 50, 58–59
Reliability, 95–96
Research, 2–3, 76
Resilience, 40, 75
Retelling, 49, 86
Rigor, 32, 36, 39–40, 86
Room arrangement, 22–23
RT. *See* Reciprocal teaching
Rubie-Davies, C., 11, 33
Rules, 25, 33, 65, 67

Scaffolding, 9, 13, 34, 55, 68, 93–94, 95
Scarcella, R., 64
School calendar, 3
Science, 11, 50, 76, 94
Self-regulation, 21, 58, 76–77
Shared agreements, 25–26
Sight cards, 38, 89
Sight word recognition, 38
Small groups, 27–28, 68–69, 85
Social and emotional learning, 25

Social purpose, 55–56
SOLOM (Student Oral Language Observation Matrix), 87–88, 93, 101–103
Spacing, 91
Spanish language, 66–67
Stamina, 37–39, 41, 43
Standards, 16, 48–50, 51
Strategic thinking, 38–39
Structure, 7, 27, 53, 55, 63, 72
Struggle, 39–40
Student Oral Language Observation Matrix. *See* SOLOM
Syntax, 53, 55, 68, 90

Teacher behavior, 32, 46
Teacher clarity, 46–47, 50, 59, 63
Teacher modeling, 77
Teasing, 26
Test of Language Development, 87
Test sample, 94
Testing, 8, 79, 81, 93
Translanguaging, 9

U.S. Department of Education, 8

Validity, 95–96
Verbs, 49–50
Vernacular English (VE), 65
Visibility, 22–23
Vietnamese language, 66–67
Visible Learning, 1–2, 4
Vocabulary, 38, 53, 55, 68, 84–85, 87

War, 6, 15
Wegerif, R., 71
WIDA (World-class Instructional Design and Assessment), 8–9, 16, 48
Word sequences, 91–93
Work-avoidant, 75
Working memory, 37
World-class Instructional Design and Assessment. *See* WIDA

Zone of proximal development (ZPD), 67

CORWIN
A SAGE Publishing Company

Helping educators make the greatest impact

CORWIN HAS ONE MISSION: to enhance education through intentional professional learning.

We build long-term relationships with our authors, educators, clients, and associations who partner with us to develop and continuously improve the best evidence-based practices that establish and support lifelong learning.